# BEYOND THE WORD

The Multiple Gestures
of Tradition

## BY THE SAME AUTHOR

POETRY:

*Quiet Violence* (1970)
*The Other Silence* (1973)
*The Old Man in Summer* (1975)
*The Jester and Other Poems* (1979)
*The Songs of Kubja and Other Poems* (1980)
*Selected Poems* (1986)
*Death of Krishna and Other Poems* (1991)
*A Morning of Rain and Other Poems* (1991)

TRIBAL POETRY:

*The Empty Distance Carries* (1972)
*The Wooden Sword* (1973)
*Staying is Nowhere* (1975)
*Forgive the Words* (1976)
*Bakhen: Ritual Invocation Songs of a Primitive Community* (1979)
*Men, Pattern of Dust* (1981)
*The Awakened Wind: Oral Poetry of the Indian Tribes* (1983)
*The Endless Weave: Tribal Songs and Tales of Orissa* (1991)
*Unending Rhythms: Oral Poetry of the Indian Tribes* (1992)

CRITICISM:

*The Curve of Meaning* (1974)
*Barefoot into Reality* (1975)
*Gestures of Intimacy* (1976)
*Bhima Bhoi* (1983)
*Modernisation and Ritual* (1986)
*Tradition and the Modern Artist* (1987)
*Mahabharata and Modern Indian Literature* (1988)
*Jagannath Dasa* (1990)
*Tribal Wall Paintings of Orissa* (1991)
*Tribal Life and Culture of Orissa* (1991)

TRANSLATION AND EDITION:

*Orissa: Kunst and Kultur in Nordost-Indian* (1980)
Ed. with Eberhard Fischer and D. Pathy.
*Longing for the South: An Anthology of Modern Macedonian Poetry* (1982)
Ed. with J. T. Boskovski.
*'Oriya Poetry Today', in Indian Poetry Today*, Vol. 3 (1982)
*Ants and Other Stories* by Gopinath Mohanty (1983)
*An Anthology of Modern Oriya Poetry* (1983)
*Folkways in Religion: Gods, Spirits and Men* (1983)
*Amaru Satakam: The Erotic Love Poetry of Amaru* (1985)
Trans. from the Sanskrit.
*The Rock and Sandalwood Tree: Modern Vietnamese Poetry* (1985)
*The Realm of the Sacred:*
Verbal Symbolism and Ritual Structure (1991)

# BEYOND THE WORD

## The Multiple Gestures of Tradition

SITAKANT MAHAPATRA

MOTILAL BANARSIDASS PUBLISHERS
PRIVATE LIMITED • DELHI

*First Edition: Delhi, 1993*



ISBN: 81-208-1108-9

Also available at:
MOTILAL BANARSIDASS
41 U.A., Bungalow Road, Jawahar Nagar, Delhi 110 007
120 Royapettah High Road, Mylapore, Madras 600 004
16 St. Mark's Road, Bangalore 560 001
Ashok Rajpath, Patna 800 004
Chowk, Varanasi 221 001

PRINTED IN INDIA
BY JAINENDRA PRAKASH JAIN AT SHRI JAINENDRA PRESS, A-45 NARAINA, PHASE I, NEW DELHI 110 028 AND PUBLISHED BY NARENDRA PRAKASH JAIN FOR MOTILAL BANARSIDASS PUBLISHERS PRIVATE LIMITED, BUNGALOW ROAD, DELHI 110 007

# Contents

# Introduction

For a long time sociologists, critics of art and literature as well as creative writers and artists have spoken of the 'modern' and the 'post-modern'. In fact the use of these terms have also become a hallmark of learned discourse on contemporary culture. Rarely 'modern' and 'post-modern' have been viewed in an evolutionary time-frame positing our times as the focal point of reference. For no 'modern' or 'post-modern' exists in complete isolation from the memory of what has gone before it. A broad, and rather inexact but generic, name for that memory is tradition. And it is tradition that needs to be viewed not merely as a continuity and counter-point to individual talent as Eliot sought to do but also in relation to the 'socialisation' of ideas and creative arts that define for each age the modern and the post-modern. The return of various art-forms to 'primitive' inspirations or to earlier centuries; the search for roots and true belongingness in an earlier idiom, image, line or refrain is not just accidental. It is perhaps the agonised attempt of our times to seek a new validation for ideas, idioms and forms which desperately seek stable anchorage. Heritage and tradition are not fashionable words. They are the not very rigid and perhaps for that reason itself, the most important parameters that define contemporaneous creativity and their linkages.

Tradition speaks through myriad gestures and in different forms. In literature, in painting, in music, in dance, in ideology. It may force us to look back, not in anger but in anxiety and concern, in affection and a yet-inarticulate sense of belonging, to what has gone before us. May be it is still possible to look on earth as our mother; to think that the epic is only a manifestation of shared destiny; to become aware that aesthetics has no greater permanence than the changing patterns of lived life; and that more and more, as art asserts the primacy of the person, we discover unsuspected truths and valid perception in 'other cultures'; in earlier centuries, in forgotten forms, in the orality of various traditions and in the archetypes in which each age finds its own special image.

The essays in this anthology seek to look at the multiple gestures of tradition in relation to our own times and in doing that have a relevance for the continuing debate on modern and post-modern.

# 1 Changing Aesthetics in Contemporary Visual Art

WRITING in 1911, Allen Upward, poet, novelist and author of *The Divine Mystery* said: "It is a sign of the times that so many of us should be busy studying the signs of the times. In no other age since the birth of Christianity has there been manifested the same devouring curiosity about the future and the same disposition to *expect a new earth*, if not a new heaven."[1] As we go into the last decade of this century and the new millennium knocks at the door, perhaps this could be an even more telling description of our generation and our times. Beyond existentialism, beyond depth psychology, beyond the hovering dark clouds of apocalypse, beyond all the talks of *angst*, despair, rootlessness, non-belonging and nausea; beyond the discovery of the new frontiers of the human mind and journey back into time for our anthropological roots, there still remains the same *devouring curiosity* about the future and what it holds; to know of things, objects and feelings which still mystify us and seem to withhold their true nature. With the ever-expanding horizon of knowledge we seem to understand less and less with each passing day. After the hubris brought about by our belief in our omniscience, and omnipotence to unravel all mystery and in the ever onward march of progress inspired by the new frontiers of science and technology, we faced the nemesis not only in two World Wars but the blankness in our knowledge, the awareness of black holes, naked singularities and the edges of the infinity over there in space and the ever-eluding mystery of life even in the tiniest cell. There is a growing feeling, which is articulated in the literature and philosophy of the last fifty years that not only we seem to know less and less of less and less each day but that 'what is said is not said, the unsaid is unsayable'. This feeling of helplessness has gone far beyond Yeats's 'the centre cannot hold' and Eliot's 'end of the endless journey to no end'. As Octavio Paz writes: "I have nothing to say, no one has anything to say, nothing and nobody except the blood,/nothing except this coming and going of the blood, this writing over the written, the repetition of the same word in mid-poem,/syllables of time, broken letters, splotches of ink, blood that goes and comes and says nothing and carries me with it."[2]

So the ideology of despair has brought about a new helplessness to the writer and the artist of our times. It has not always been a fashionable despair or a mask of cynicism. It has gone deep as canker into the soul of our civilization. The traumatic developments in society around us, the rhythms of violence and uncertainty, the orchestrated denial of the possibility of human creativity and its apparent meaninglessness faced with the indifference of a cruel universe, all these have combined to create a sense of utter despair. Technology and science have brought us only to a new awareness of our ignorance. As Eliot would say: 'Endless invention, endless experiment,/brings knowledge of motion, but not of stillness, knowledge of speech but not of silence'. Man has almost lost his bearings. The horrors of loneliness, the invasion of material objects into the psyche, (we remember the Sartre character Roquentin's nausea watching the snarled roots of a tree) the fear of the machine and the progressive loss of grip on its expanding realm, the emergence of the megalopolises of glass-concrete jungle—all of these have conspired to give a sense of the dehumanisation of life and a deep craving to find a measure of balance, a still centre where human creativity is still the determinant of meaning and value both for the individual and society. The rejection of all traditional and renaissance concepts and life-views have led to a major crisis of confidence and attempts to find refuge in a variety of experimentations seeking to break up the veneer of placid stability and look beyond the gentility principle. Artists have used a wide variety of objects and materials—from torn carpets to bones, wood chips, mud, metal or whatever, to create the effect of mixed-up perspectives in life through traumatic collages. The gestures of passion, violence, hatred and bloodshed have led some to allow the flow of paint to determine perspective and lines. Ambivalences, contradictions, violent impulses have been sought to be conveyed through the interacting patterns in a canvas. Sometimes the canvas has appeared to be exploding out of itself in the dissolution of paint; at other times optical illusions have been sought to be created. The satires on serious art through travesties and anti-art postures only indicate the varying visions of contemporary reality and the visual artists' occasionally compulsive response to it. In the hands of the less mature these *avant-garde* techniques may sometimes tend to degenerate into stylistic gimmicks and shallow posturings. But in the hands of the serious-minded they are only various streams of revolt against the dehumanisation of our times and the way of saying no to the darkness of today. All of these can be seen as only parts of a desperate search for meaning and relevance. The interest in Yoga, Tantra, Zen, levels of consciousness, forms of ecstasy has also its manifestations in new patterns of perspective and collage. The more serious among these new searches through alternative modes of experience have sought to explore the inner life of our times by reaching out to our roots and by denying the overpowering effects of the mechanisation of life that brings fatigue and boredom as the final result. They seek answers to the riddle of life and the quotidian living in our times. They try to discover archetypes or conglomerate symbols for this destiny to be man on this planet, enmeshed in the myriad nets of falsehood and mask. In an interview Sam Francis, the painter once said, "Each painting is like my body-print, taken at different moments in my life". Many have turned to the spiritual philosophies of the East and the Primitive societies for their source of inspiration. Many like Charles Seliger, Onslow Ford, Morris Graves and Lee Mullican have gone back in their own ways, to Paul Klee's belief that the visible world is "merely an isolated case in relation to the universe and that there are many more other, latent realities".[3]

The artist is face to face with the great blankness and there is an obsessive feeling that perhaps he will never find that word, that stroke of the brush, that mudra or gesture that will once again convey what he means to convey. The pen mutinies, the brush revolts, feelings freeze and it becomes an endless search to regain confidence, faith and composure.

But with the *devouring curiosity* to know what the future holds, the artist and writer would not, however, give up the hope of a new earth, if not a new heaven. For this is the only earth he is privileged to know; the only one to savour in the little time allotted to him between birth and death. So the here and the now are all that matters. May be there was never a heaven, may be this earth itself was the only heaven; may be the gods never existed except in the human imagination and in any case most of them were dead and can be resurrected only with human will. So it is only a new earth that is to be created, a new earth pregnant with human hopes and desires, eloquent with the erotic and the sensuous, the dust and the dream of man. A new earth with all its sun-laden promises, where the rivers speak to men in their sleep as they flow on to sea and the silent hills hint at forgotten meanings. And a new man whose words are his flesh and the colours and lines on the canvas his soul, where each gesture of his hand is his ultimate craving, his final dream.

Yes, it was to be a new earth, an earth that is seen by the new-born with eyes of wonder. A new earth re-born for man each new day with a new sun-rise. Isms no longer mattered in art and literature. We had seen all of them. They merely tried to give shape to the shapeless, tone to the toneless and ascribe meaning to all the meaninglessness of this world. Yes, isms had never mattered to the true artist. Whether he handled words, stones, metal, canvas or his voice, isms never mattered. They were mere intellectual formalities, ideologies based on logic and rationalisation. And aesthetics was only a distorted way of looking at creativity as a process and the created as the artefact, be it a poem, a painting, a piece of music or a movement in space as a gesture. And it is not merely that we know of the figure that a poem makes, or the words that a painting whispers in our ears or the colours that flash out of the proliferation of a *raga* or an overture and the stars which fly away in the gyration of a rhythmic fury in a dance. We also know that aesthetics as an intellectual response to the corpus of human creativity hardly ever did justice to the 'created' or the creative process; that at its best it had to stop at the gate of the ultimate mystery—the human imagination as the source of all creativity. Aesthetics as the theoretical study of the arts and 'related types of behaviour and experience' has travelled a long and somewhat arid distance from the idea of beauty in Plato's *Symposium* to our times. Plato was not unaware of the grandeur of Greek Poetry or sculpture. But he emphasised a different vision of beauty which, by implication, was missed by previous poets, painters and sculptors. In Plato the essential nature of beauty reveals itself to the enraptured beholder who ascends from the admiration of physical perfection to the discovery of inward beauty and then to an ultimate vision. This happens because the true beholder is guided by love (*eros*). The beautiful had for him a quality that was 'nonsensuous, transcendent splendour' and it was to be described only by certain negations: it was not subject to growth and decays; was not like a bodily frame, not mutable or enmeshed in relativities. It was, on the other hand, 'being itself by itself'. The negative science of beauty was, however, linked to an act of participation by the beholder where 'sensuousness' was not denied. Plato did view poetry (as much as painting) as closely linked to the erotic vision of beauty. The poet, Plato made Socrates say in the *phaedrus* and the *Ion* and he could have also spoken the same of the painter, 'chants his praises in *sacred madness*'.

It is true the Greek language had no word corresponding to our concept of 'art' with its aesthetic overtones. Hence it would be idle to look for an aesthetic theory of art in Plato. But Plato associated art with imitation or mimesis, a word which for the Greek was close to 're-anactment' than 'copying'. Mimesis had a constructive power. Plato was also a believer in the Pythagorean theory of music that believed that the same numeric harmony that is "audible through music also determines the order of the universe as well as that of the soul".

Aesthetics in our times has long given up its claim to establish any universal discourse for appreciating beauty or giving us a law or a system of values relating to it. It has taken on the more humble and more pedestrian task of helping us understand the sources of creativity and the nature of the creative process; the contours, the parameters, the processes and the configurations of the experiences that are characterised as aesthetic. It has also been treated partly as a problem in semantics and often no particular answer has been forthcoming as to what indeed is an aesthetic experience or the special quality of an object that stimulates such experience.

The sensuous and the abstract, the erotic and the sublime ideational, the clay and the star perhaps remain interwoven in any object of beauty or the stimulation which it has for us. Kant and German aesthetic theory had over-emphasised the metaphysical and the transcendental elements in its search for the *a priori* and universal principles of aesthetic value and beauty. It was against that, that others emphasised the element of 'fine frenzy' or a revised version of *sacred madness* which found its extreme spokesman finally in Rimbaud when he advocated the 'derangement of the senses' as the vital element of creativity.

Beyond this there is also the question of the audience, the beholder, the viewer, the listener and the reader. The meaning of a painting, a poem or an orchestra does not begin and end with what the artist conveys or intended to convey. It continues its progressive act of realisation in the experience of its audience. This is why the true meaning of a piece of art is never completed or fully realised because its audience remains a continuity in the flux of time and for all ages. Besides, the appreciation of the outside reality—the object, the artefact, the words, the canvas or the sound—is intimately linked to the feeling, the mood of the agent, the climate of his heart. Each theoretician on aesthetics has to say as much on the outer as the inner reality that go to the making of art and its aesthetic enjoyment. People have spoken of aesthetics 'from below' as derived from observation and pragmatic analysis as distinct from aesthetics 'from above' based on ideas and metaphysics. We have also heard of empirical depth psychology analysing creative impulses and of the sociology of literary and artistic imagination.

The revolutionary change in viewing art objects changed with access to different forms of art—Western and Eastern, modern and primitive, the art objects of Asia, Pacific and Africa. There was not only greater sampling of art objects and their varying genesis of creativity now available for comparison but scholars, critics and artists themselves had access to different theories of beauty and theories of art.

Petrarch, that early embodiment of post-medieval man once ascended the Mont Ventoux and stood transfixed by the grandeur of the Panorama. He is reported to have opened the copy of St. Augustin's *Confessions* which he always used to carry with him and the first lines which caught his eyes were those which exhorted readers not to forget the beauty of their inner being, the 'interior landscape', in seeking beauty in the external reality: "And men go to wonder at mountain heights . . .and leave themselves behind". It is not very different in tone from what Mark Tobey the modern American painter says: "the dimension that counts for the creative person is the space he creates within himself. This inner space is closer to the infinite than the other, and it is the privilege of a balanced mind . . . to be as aware of inner space as he is of outer space. If he ventures in one, and neglects the other, man falls of his horse and the equilibrium is broken."[4] It is not a question of mysticism or the spiritual. It is basically a question of the imagination and the visions of inner space which have inspired all great art at all times.

Perhaps in our times the pendulum has swung so much towards the machine, the quotidian, the routinised experience, and the dehumanising influence of habit and automatism that the need for emphasising the inner vision and inner reality has been felt all the more. The emphasis on the objective and detached treatment of themes and objects, events and emotions have gone so far that some years ago Morris Graves, in opposition to it, gave us that rallying cry 'subjective *is* objective'. There is a growing belief that true subjectivity can be the only objectivity possible in our world. There have been interest in various non-Western theories of aesthetics like *rasa* and *dhvani*. Anandavardhana in his *Dhvanyaloka*[5] (which has been translated as the Light of Suggestion) and Abhinavagupta in his *Locana* (The Eye) gave us new insight as to the way extremely subtle suggestions and suggestiveness are the hallmark of great literature (and the same could easily be applied also to painting) and analysed the psychological backdrop to the making of such *suggestiveness*.

There have also been talks of the 'pure instant' and 'pure psychic automatism'. There has been talk of 'painting in the instant', where the artist disappears for a moment and reappears in the painting once again. Nature is being recognised once again as primordial, as the essential ingredient of the inscape that is only the other name of inner space and inner time. Sam Francis and Gordon Onslow Ford and others who took on ideas from André Breton and went far beyond him, emphasise principles which in the literary context was given to us by Baudelaire and Rimbaud. In fact Kandinsky spoke as much in his *On the Spiritual in Art*: "An artist who sees that the imitation of natural appearances, however artistic, is not for him, the kind of creative artist who wants to express his own inner world, sees with envy how naturally and easily such goals can be attained in music, the least *material* of the arts today. It is understandable if he turns towards it and tries to find the same means in his own art. Hence the current search for rhythm in painting, for mathematical, abstract construction, the value placed today upon the repetition of coloured tones, the way colours are set in motion. . ."[6] What Kandinsky wrote in 1912 has assumed even greater importance as the years have rolled by.

Aesthetics has come to emphasise the autonomy of the universe of artistic creativity, an autonomy that is engaged in a culpable rivalry with God. For in a sense no true artist ever tolerates reality. The world is a poor sketch by uninvisible God that deserves and demands recreating, reworking, resketching. It is, however, not the product of a totally mental inscape. It is also inhabited by the creatively conceived events and objects which are the varying elements of the artist's response to the world he lives in. No longer the artist seeks a meaning outside his canvas. Painting like poetry, like music now insists that it should not mean but *be*. And its being is the inner soul of the creative artist and not a mimesis or a recreation, let alone a copy. This is the ultimate meaning of the subjective being the true objective of which Morris Graves has spoken about.

The task of all art—poetry, painting, sculpture, music—is to express the internal. This 'internal' could be the artist's innermost thoughts and feelings. It could also be a mysterious reality which lies beyond or behind the outward appearance of things. This has often led to a kind of growing-together of the arts. Painters, writers, composers, sculptors have taken greater interest in one another's medium and form perhaps more than ever before. This is a development that has an enormous and perhaps healthy influence on the arts. This recalls another time when composers like Schoenerg painted; painters like Kandinsky and Kokoschka wrote plays and poems and playwrights like Barlach also sculpted.

One other development which has also had a profound influence on the changing aesthetic of visual arts is the revival of the memory of childhood and the primitive vision of life—two aspects which seem to give a great deal of hope and courage to the troubled psyche of our times. The child as the archetypal symbol of innocence and a sense of wonder, of the desire to possess the world in one mighty sweep, and of the element of play in life has variously haunted our times. Echoing Huizinga who spoke of us the *homo sapien* as basically *homo luden* or man the player, scholars have tried to treat the play element as the crucial element in artistic creativity. It has further been held that in the true artist the child lives on until his death and does not die prematurely as in others. The child in every artist is indeed the creator. It is also held that the cry of every new-born is yet another proof that god has still not lost hope of man. It is an assertion of the continuity of our childhood, the assertion that we can still see, wide-eyed and full of wonder, as if we are witnessing the world's first sunrise and sunset, its first birth and death. Modern artists have also gone back to the art of the primitive communities where the vital, the intuitive and the raw come through as stark, naked and unadorned realities. In fact the child and the primitive world view perhaps hold something in common: the totality of grasp on reality, the sense of pristine wonder and a total purity of expression. This view is based on the belief that there can be no consolation for the inevitability of decay and death in a supposedly blissful rebirth in an imaginary 'other world' or an abstract world of the mind. Renewal is here and now, in this world, in the quickly fading blossoms of the forests, in the transience of love and the charmed instant and the primitive and pure innocence of our children. Most of the ceremonies and rituals of the primitive world are vegetative ceremonies and rituals of fecundity. And they flow from the basic realisation of the fecundity of life and not its drying up. They centre round a total and autonomous quality which is beyond the binary oppositions of pleasure and pain, heaven and hell, good and evil, sacred and profane.

This resurgence or this return to the mythology of the child and the primitive is partly a swing away from too much of adulthood, too exact a knowledge; a retreat from and a no to what Denman Ross had asserted: "no art can be satisfactorily practised without constant reference and obedience to mathematical principles, systems or laws"[7] or what in another context Maratta had echoed: "to produce harmony in a work of art we must use *numbers, metrology, the science of measuring* as all bodies and emotions are subject to numerical calculations".[8]

There are some who believed and emphasised like de Zayas, and Robert Coady the strong relationship between the work of such primitive races as the African Negroes . . . the Mexican Indians and the art of today. Primitive art was considered important because "it is the most adaptable to the expression of feelings being essentially the imaginative forms, and also the most simple and direct. Primtive art is most closely related to the feelings".[9]

But was a return to the true roots of primitive world view possible any longer? The basic quality of child and primitive world view is their vitality, their un-selfconscious and fully natural expression. Can the modern artist really enter into that charmed universe with all his naivemania and primitology, as he is all the time only too conscious of his times and his designed return to that primal innocence is after all only a strategy to arrive at consolation or grace, and another mode of regaining vitality and authenticity. In trying to be the child may he not produce 'childish art'? For unlike the child or the primitive, the modern artist, as de Zayas asserts, "is the prototype of consciousness. He works premeditatedly, he dislocates, he disharmonises, exaggerates . . . He is an ecletic in spirit and iconoclast in action".[10]

It is true there is a difficulty here though more and more artists of the Western world have, for quite some time now, turned to the art of the primitive communities spread all over the world. This is also equally true of the Third World countries where the creative surge in visual arts and the critical idiom in which such art is to be viewed were not a little influenced by Western creative and critical categories at least in the earlier decades. But slowly the pale reflection of visions and idioms elsewhere have given place to authentic and pulsating local idioms and colour and the search for roots both in the tradition of the centuries and of the preliterate primitives of their own countries. The heritage of the West was, of course, a universal heritage and there was neither a need nor an obsession to fly away from it or consciously deny or denigrate it. On the other hand, the return to roots was essentially a recreation of tradition, a new vision of the ancient dreams, a new renewal. After all, the boundaries of tradition constantly keep changing and expanding. When Zayas simplistically pronounced that 'Art is dead' he did not realise that what was dead was perhaps precisionism, the compulsion to experiment with abstract art and that perhaps that was only a new beginning to recover new grounds of vitality and immediacy, of innocence and wonder that had been lost in the craze for scientism and abstraction.

A motto for the changing aesthetics in visual arts could well be the inscription on Josef Olbrich's building for the Secession Group in Vienna way back in 1898: To the time its art/to art its freedom. At that time it was a motto partly based on the vision of Romanticism and partly that of Baudelaire. But it still retains its validity. Art in our troubled times, with its technological compulsions, its ennui and fatigue, its violence and turbulence, its manic depressions and terrors, its grandeurs and its defeats, its ecstasies and despairs—has truly expressed itself in myriad forms and colours, new visions and insights and through new cultural polarities like the *empathetic* and the *abstract* (Wilhelm Worringer) or the *vital* and the *geometric*.

In various modes and flowing in multitude of streams visual art of our times has been both creating and rediscovering its changing aesthetics. It has refused to be imprisoned by any ism. It has tried to be more human, to have the most intense content and yet not to be totally divorced from the world of ordinary men and society with all its humdrum reality and the un-romantic, non-sensational drabness of the daily ritual of living. Life's grandeur and cruelty, its dullness and dream, its clay and its stars, all of them have had a relevance for the new aesthetic. Its hearth is in those zones of the psyche where images are born and its prayer that these anguished but pure images partake of all of man's fears and hopes, all his ugliness and beauty, his madness and his divinity.

The talk of 'a loss of centre' heard after the Second World War, the attacks of Wyndham Lewis and Wiedle, the hesitation and hopes in writers like Camus and Gottfied Benn, the tragic vision of Franz Marc the Fritz Winter's *Driving Forces of the Earth*, the intuitive and integrative vision of Kandinsky, Klee, Mondrian and Picasso and a host of other developments only provide the backdrop to the shaping of this new aesthetic. The tragedy of our times was not only the haunting images of death or darkness or of loss of hope and brooding melancholy as in Van Gogh's painting of crows over a field of golden wheat. The even greater tragedy was more poignantly brought out in his other painting where a group of men were going round and round in a circle in the closed semi-darkness of a room while outside there was moonlight and breeze and all that they needed to do was to throw open the door and go out. Van Gogh deeply loved the "heavy, dark, solid tone of the earth and men with earthbound gestures". He was attracted by the reality of things, their silent eloquence. In 1882, when he first tired his hand at landscape painting, he was not in the least concerned with the picture, the scenery, or with natural appearance. Instead he was interested only in the 'enormous power and solidity of the soil'. That was what he wanted to make visible. He flung his energies "into the things of this earth with the unrestrained religious fervour which always characterised him".

Van Gogh's artistic vision and his destiny have deeply influenced the history and aesthetics of modern visual art. Here was a vision that wanted to render the *truth of the things.* Literally he had seen the soul of the materials, of the roots of the trees, the irises, the corn fields, the crows. He had read and understood the metaphysics of the physical. In fact he squeezed roots and trees directly out of his tubes and modelled with his brush. In a letter to his alter ego, his brother Theo he wrote, 'when you want to grow you must plunge into the earth'. And plunge he did to the point of drowning. As Werner Haftmann would say "he dug deeper and deeper, in constant search of images which are contained in things, and yet at the same time lie beind them

... he bored into the faces of the witched peasants around him, drawing like one possessed, ... to discover ... that which lies behind the individual face, the great mask of human suffering".[11]

His destiny was linked in a way to his vision: to tear apart the yet greater mask that is death and to see what lies behind it. His Parisian friends could only half understand what they later called his 'tragic attitude' (Klee) and his pathological courting of destruction. The deep yearning for the earth and a desire to possess it, the explosion of creative energy and the failure of Gauguin's advice to him to 'paint from memory' reveal a major challenge to and response of aesthetics of modern visual art.

The modern artist has been confronted with a variety of moral, religious and social demands and his dialogue with society has sometimes led to a near-total retreat into the self or, at the other end of the spectrum, complete submergence in the group. Art is neither for a priesthood nor is it for a multitude or a crowd. The more it withdraws from the community and seems to belong only to a charmed circle of infinitely small experts, professionals and economic gate-keepers, the museum-owners and the gallery-managers—the less becomes its relevance to the times and its searing concerns. The public may be losing out somewhere even as prices of canvases keep soaring. Van Gogh sold only one painting in his life-time but today the portrait of Dr. Gachet may be auctioned for a mind-boggling 82.5 million dollars to an affluent and commercially powerful dealer. Modern art cannot isolate itself from this harsh and complex reality when the world of art, slowly but imperceptibly, is getting transformed into an art industry and when liquidity seems to be all. The richness of the visual experience of modern art—and there is no doubt at all about its immense fecundity, its range, its variety and excellence—is facing near-collapse under the brute weight of price. While excellence in any creative art—poetry, music, painting or sculpture—may not always be for the layman these are developments which modern art and its aesthetics can ill afford to ignore.

The modern artist recognises the metaphysics inherent in the physical. Each object after all possesses a soul; it is only a question of knowing how to awaken it; so that even dull inert matter begins to lisp in its unique, incomparable and compulsive idiom.

It is the same idea in poetry that E.E. Cummings celebrates in the wheelbarow in the rain. For the artist it is not merely a world in a grain of sand or eternity in an hour. It is even more. It is discovering the language of silence and the eloquence of colour. It is discovering the throbbing heart of inert matter and being able to listen to it and give it a shape.

The new aesthetic emphasises that in painting, as in poetry or music we should look for no meaning outside the canvas. The ideology, the thematic content, the humanistic concern *behind* a painting are all of secondary significance, if not altogether irrelevant. A painting, after all, is only a *concrete event*, a celebration of an instant of realisation.

Perhaps in the celebration of this event colour now takes a place more seminal, more central than form, that other centrepiece of earlier centuries. The anguished search for pure colour and its sonorous organisation is a major hallmark of the new aesthetic. In fact the realisation seems to be that colour after all is itself form, that it combines both the sensuous and the abstract, the esoteric and the familiar, the primitive impulse and the most sophisticated cognition, the social landscape as also the psyche of the mind. Colour has both luminosity and rhythm. It is abstraction, it is also concrete. In fact it gives intimation both of the greater reality and the greater abstraction towards which modern painting has moved on over the years. Colour is no longer a vehicle: neither the qualitative garment as in concrete painting nor the qualitative mood of the ground as in Abstract Expressionism. Modern Art has indeed travelled a long way from the days of Kandinsky and Delauney and their improvisation and Orphist construction. In fact the attitude to colour had gone through all the stages from Gauguin's 'pure colour' and its delineation in Kandinsky's early period through the developments from Cezanne to Juan Gris, from Nay and Sam Francis to the invasion of Eastern imageries from Japan and the primitive peoples. Colour contains the magical, the mythical, the lyrical and even the animistic. It is in fact an escape route into the primitive psyche from the oppression of excessive intellectual cerebration. This new approach to colour has perhaps helped maintain a balance between logical vigour and intense passion that has characterised so much of modern painting.

Van Gogh had shared with Gauguin and Seurata belief in the infinite potential of pure colour and line to express not only external reality but moods and events. The 'terrible human passions', for him could be conveyed by colour. For example the Cafe at Arles at night is a place where a man can lose his mind and commit crimes and the colours bring out the dark powers that rule over a man's sleep.

It was many years ago this author had composed a small poem as his humble tribute to Van Gogh, the painter whose life and vision have perhaps made one of the greatest impacts on the modern artist's vision of creative art. I crave your indulgence to read out that poem entitled 'The Painter':

From pores of his skin
multiple suns swim away
cancelling the sonorous sky;
valleys in meditation look back in astonished silence
hills hint at forgotten distances
breathless in the cumulus of meaning.

Colour is only the arithmetic of ancient anguish
shattering clear air and the incandescent sun
mindlessly;
Moon's tricky handiwork only too obvious
as scattered on the landscape
unmasked pains
mimick a slow dance.

Linear flames
converging on darkness
welding deaths and dreams
relating time to a hypothesis
and shapes to a toneles foliage.

Painter Emerson Woelffer once tried to list the elements and states of being that provoked his work. His tentative list ran somewhat like this: chance, time, anger, order, black, memory, love, night, silence, music, automatism, humour, poetry, sorrow, passion, chaos, intuition, accident, obsession, irrationality, the unknown.

Would that not be broadly a list of the elements of the changing aesthetics, the varying vision of contemporary art and what goes with it?

The aesthetics of the visual arts in our times has thus many facets. It reveals an attempt to reconcile many binary oppositions: the opposition of committed art *vrs* art of detachment; the emphasis on the myth of reality and the flight from it; the possibilities of the lyrical tradition as against the hermetic; the concrete and the expressive *vrs* the abstract and the psychic; the dilemma of opposition between form and colour; art as meditation on the self *vrs* art as a horde of destruction, and the spiritual intimations of the inner eye *vrs* metaphysics of the physical.

Western art and Western life-style may have, at least on the surface, destroyed a number of ancient cultures and their world views and approach to reality but the West has not also remained insulated against the invasion of the magical world of the East and the culture of ancient civilisations and of the preliterate societies with their emphasis on the erotic and the sensuous, the dark impulses of totemism and the intuitive.

The changing aesthetic in contemporary visual arts has taken artists to all the secret recesses of the inner reality of the soul and the external reality in the outer space. It has tried to combine dream and death and in the process given a new meaning to both. It has celebrated both the pathos of our transience, the fragility of our dream and our lusty greed and intense craving for this dusty earth and its myriad grandeurs. And the modern artist's dream has been to assert, to use the lines of Octavio Paz used in another context, to continue to dream, for it is only there that both reality and responsibilities begin.

"We must sleep with open eyes, we must dream with our hands/ We must dream the dreams of a river seeking its course, of the sun dreaming its worlds/we must dream aloud, we must sing till the song puts forth roots, trunk, branches, birds, star/ We must sing till the dream engenders in the sleeper's flank the red wheat-ear of resurrection/the womanly water, the spring at which we may drink and recognise ourselves and recover/the spring that tells us we are men, the water that speaks alone in the night and calls us by name"—from The Broken Waterjar.[13]

Yes modern art's dream is to baptise itself at that sacred spring that tells us again and again that we are men, we are men.

[Keynote Address opening the VII Triennale of Arts
New Delhi, 1991 January]

## NOTES

1. Upward, Allen (1910) 'The New Age' in the Journal of the same name edited by A.R. Orage.
2. Paz, Octavio (1979) *Selected Poems*, Penguin, Middlesex England, p. 35.
3. Klee, Paul (1959) "Creative Credo" (1920) in *The Inward Vision:. Water-colours, Drawings and Writings* by Paul Klee, New York, Abrams.
4. Tobey Mark (1961) Quoted in *Retrospective Mark Tobey*, Musee des Arts Decoratifs, Palais du Louvre.
5. Daniel H.H. Ingalls (ed.) (1990) *Dhvanyaloka of Anandvardhana with the Locana* of Abhinavagupta, Harvard University Press, Cambridge, USA, Harvard Oriental Series, Vol. 49.
6. Kandinsky (1912) *On the Spiritual in Art*, Munich, 2nd Edition.
7. Ross, D.W. (1919) *The Painter's Palette: A Theory of Tone Relations: An Instrument of Expression*, Boston/New York quoted by Milton W. Browne, *American Painting from the Armoury Show to the Depression*, Princeton 1955, p. 161.
8. Maratta, H.G. (1955) 'A Rediscovery of the Principles of Form Measurement' *Arts and Decoration* quoted by Browne 1955, p. 161.
9. Zayas, Marius de and Haviland, Paul (1913) *A Study of the Modern Evolution of Plastic Expression*, New York, p. 11.
10. Zayas, Marius de (1912) 'The Sun has Set', *Camera Work*, No. 39.
11. Haftmann, Werner (1960) *Painting in the Twentieth Century*, London (Translation: Ralph Manheim), p. 26.
12. *Ibid.*, p. 26.
13. Paz, Octavio (1979) *Selected Poems*, Penguin Middlesex, England, p. 29.

# 2 | Tribal Art of Orissa

WHILE ORISSA's tribal art and culture share certain universal characteristics common to all pre-literate and primitive cultures, it has also certain special features determined by the historical circumstances of the region which is modern Orissa. In terms of historical experience this region remained fairly isolated from the sweep of invasions and the imperial traditions which determined cultural patterns in North India to a large extent. It was also one of the last regions to go under British rule. This has made possible the retention of traditional cultural forms in a comparatively purer, undistorted and original form. Secondly, it led to the evolution of a composite culture which is a remarkable continuum of classical, folk and tribal elements. Scholars feel that the tribal origin of Lord Jagannath at Puri is a distinct possibility. Apart from prevailing legends, the anthropomorphic wooden figure of the deity, looking half-formed, incomplete and bland, does resemble the human figures in wood made by some tribal communities. The *chaau* dance of Mayurbhanj has distinct elements of classical Orissi, local folk and Santal dance forms particularly the Dantha and the Dasain. The Vedic Rudra and the Puranic Siva become the village deity Mahadev. And the Santal God Maran-buru is not very unlike this 'easily-pleased' god (Asutosha) who is the giver of gifts. Orissa's tribal art and culture thus needs to be viewed as a part of the composite continuum that is Orissan culture.

Simultaneously Orissa's tribal art has also certain characteristics which is common to all primitive art. It is functional and utilitarian and is not the product of the leisured activity of a privileged group or class. It is enither created by a small elite, often resembling an exclusive priesthood, nor is it meant for *vicarious* enjoyment of a few who can pay for it. It is participative, communal and integral to the business of living and dying. There is no distinction between high art and low craft. A dance number may have an expanding circle of participants as three generations join in at the unsparing call of the accompanying drum-beat. An ordinary object like a Juang comb or a Dongria Kondh tobacco pouch may have etchings which are intricately designed and laboriously carried out. Art is created as one lives and performs different activities within the community. To an extent therefore it is conventional in its patterns and rhythms and does not emphasise the creative ego of the artist or his individual inspiration. Art creation is a largely unstructured, communal activity that gives the individual a sense of fulfilment as a member of his community. The emphasis is rarely on the inspired individual ego.

Beyond the family and the community is the world of ancestors and gods and spirits. In fact the ancestors have an intimate link with the living members of the community and it is a sin to forget them on festival or ritual occasions. The village is the 'sacred soil of ancestors' who participate in the joys and sorrows of their lineage. Then there are the gods—generally forming large pantheons—both benevolent and malevolent, who have to be appropriately appeased through 'offerings' and their blessings invoked for group-welfare. The offerings include sacrificial objects and verbal invocations along with appropriate rituals. The motivation behind art creation has thus two primary sources: one functional, creating objects of daily use, etching designs on combs, painting the walls, weaving scarfs etc.; the other, religious-ritualistic meant to be part of the 'offering' to gods and ancestors.

Orissa has sixty-two tribal communities which differ widely in terms of their numbers, degree of acculturation, level of economic and educational backwardness and articulation of cultural self-image through oral literature (songs, tales, myths of creation etc.), performing traditions (songs land dances) and visual arts. Having worked nearly two decades on their oral poetry, or what is better termed as 'song-poems', this author may venture a generalisation. It is that taken as a whole the Orissa tribes have a stronger literary-performing tradition than in the field of visual arts. Among the latter the dominate activity is wall painting, both sacred and secular, both ritualistic and purely decorative. Some of them do make exquisite textile fabrics for their own use but in a rather limited scale. They are very fond of jewellery, some of which they themselves fabricate and others are made for them, in a symbiotic economic relationship, by the non-tribal people in their immediate neighbourhood. Large-sized sculptures in wood are not very common, except some done for ritual purposes. More common are the etchings, the carving on doors, windows, tabacco pouches etc. Stone sculpture is also primarily for ritualistic purposes.

Sculpting in wood, stone or metal is not a very popular activity among Orissa tribes. The doors and windows of Santals have often geometric patterns and designs of flowering creepers and animals. The windows of Juangs have sometimes intricate designs and carvings. The Kutia Kondhs carve their doors with stylised forms of birds and animals that border on the surreal. Other articles of daily use such as wooden containers, boxes, beams of houses also contain carved figures of human beings, birds and animals. The Dongria Kondhs use large-sized wooden poles, variously carved, as Dharani Pennu or Earth goddess. In each village one can come across such carved poles which are worshipped by the villagers. Sometimes they also occur in the individual household of the comparatively affluent. The Meria pillar, to which the human victim used to be tied in the sacred ritual of Meria sacrifice lasting three days in earlier times, used to be a well-carved pillar with a small death-bird perching on top. This author had seen such a pillar in an interior Kondh village nearly a decade ago. In recent times, however, it is a rather bland pillar to which the sacrificial animal is tied. The carvings are becoming rarer. The ritual is also becoming a simpler affair compared to the elaborate drinking, feasting, singing of invocation to the Earth goddess, the ritual anointing of the Meria and the dances that have been described by both Macpherson and Campbell in their Reports to the British administration while working on the assigned job of putting an end to the 'barbaric rite of human sacrifice in Kondhistan'. The Meria festival has an elaborate invocation song which is a prayer to the Earth goddess to bestow plenty of crops, ensure the good health of the community and save it from the depredation of wild animals. The Meria invocation is thus reminiscent of Vedic invocation. The Meria pillar and the Dharani Pennu pole are variously carved in different villages. The Meria sacrifice and Dharani Pennu worship is common to both the Dongria Kondhs of Koraput district and the Kutia Kondhs of Phulbani district.

It is, however, the Juangs who excel in their etchings on the combs which are of different shapes and sizes and made of either timber of bamboo. Their designs are intricate and are a mix of ritualistic and secular objects. The variety and range of depictions of the objects is simply fascinating. This small primitive group is perhaps the finest makers of combs in timber and bamboo in the whole of India. The human figures are stylised and so too are the figures of animals such as horses and elephants enclosed within spaces created by geometric designs. The Oraon and Gond tribes of Sundergarh and Sambalpur make roof-tiles with stylised human beings perched on them and *tulshi chauras* as votive objects. They also make *dolis* with the bridegroom and bride sitting inside as cute objects.

Then there are the figures of village deity carved in wood which are seen at the entrance to Kondh villages. The deity is supposed to guard the village against attacks of disease and pestilence and is placed in a small make-shift hut. But they don't have any particular significance as sculpture. The Kondhs also carve designs and panels on wooden planks and pillars incorporating ritual symbols.

The Gonds of Mayurbhanj give different shapes to solid blocks of stones by cutting and polishing and make deities out of them. Such stone menhirs representing village goddesses are placed near the root of a tree in the outskirts of the village and are worshipped. In terracotta the Gonds of Sundergarh have a measure of excellence and they make stylised figures of animals and tall multi-layered lamps, besides exquisite pitcher, bowls and other earthenwares of daily use. The Santals, the Oraons and the Hos also fabricate their earthern vessels, pitcher and containers in different shapes and sizes.

In metalware some of the tribes have excelled in the art of

*dhokra* casting though it looks certain that they initially learnt it from the neighbouring blacksmiths. The Bhuiyans of Dhenkanal and the Godabas of Koraput are now fabricating various functional objects (measures for rice, bowls, etc.) and ritualistic objects (decorative motifs with birds and animals figures). They are, however, not at significant and rarely as large as some of the *dhokra* objects made by Bastar tribals. Some of the Kondh *dhokra* castings are, however, quite significant as votive objects. They also cast men and women stylised in various forms.

The various ritualistic objects carved in stone or wood and fabricated with clay or metal, are used on different occasions of worship. Almost all the sixtytwo tribal groups have large pantheons of gods and goddesses, generally distinguished as malevolent or benevolent. Most of them are also animistic, recognising trees, rivers and hills as gods and making suitable offerings to them. In fact a very large number of votive objects in stone, wood and metal answer the requirements of religious worship both at the village level performed by the priest or at the family level performed by the head of the household.

In textiles it is the Dongrias, the Gadabas and the Santals who create a small range of exquisite designs with locally fabricated looms. The Dongria scarfs, which both men and women use to cover the upper part of the body, have exquisite traditional designs and have a beautiful mix of colour. The Santal textile is more sophisticated in design and use a larger range of coloured threads. The Gadabas mix cotton yarns with the yarns made out of bark of a local tree and the sarees, with only two or three colour stripes, woven on locally fabricated looms, is the traditional dress of Gadaba women. The Bondas too weave their tiny loin-cloth used by the women on very small looms which they themselves fabricate.

The tribal communities of Orissa reveal a strong impulse to adorn their bodies with a variety of jewellery. The women are extremely fond of jewellery of various types and in some cases, as among the Dongrias, the men are also very fond of them. The most outstanding example of 'heavy' jewellery is that of the Bonda women. The women with shaven heads are also topless and wear only a very small and flimsy cloth loosely tied round the waist. But a large number of brass collars and coloured bead necklaces round the neck go down even below the navel and thus cover the entire upper part of the body. It is mostly heavy collars of brass which sometimes go up to seven numbers round the neck of a single woman. They also wear brass rings on the fingers and a waistband or girdle made of brass or iron bugles which keeps the flimsy strip of loin-cloth in place. Round her shaven head the Bonda woman wears a number of bands of simple palmyra strips or woven and plaited fillets. Into these bands the younger girls stick flowers and the older women their leaf-pipes. While the brass collars are purchased from local blacksmiths the head dress and the colourful bead necklaces are made by the Bondas themselves. The necklaces use glass beads, shells and beans and mostly they are in green, blue, ochre and yellow colours. The Bonda women also wear a number of brass bangles separated by rings of old cloth so as to prevent them from rubbing against each other.

The Dongrias are perhaps the most colourful when it comes to ornaments of both men and women. While Bondas generally don't use ornaments on the nose and ear, Dongria men and women wear a large number of various types of rings on the ear-lobes and nose. Their bead necklaces are also more exquisitely made and there is a fine blending of colours. The jewellery used by the Kondh women for their head is also exquisite, blending neatly with the hanging circular coins and the stylised coiffure. Among the Gadaba women's jewellery, apart from the necklaces of coloured beads, is the very large ear-rings. Along with their sarees which they themselves weave these bead-necklaces and large ear-rings give a distinctive look to the Gadaba women.

The Saoras, the Santals, the Parajas and in fact most of the tribal communities are equally fond of jewellery. Apart from necklaces of beads these are in aluminium, brass and sometimes copper. Necklaces of coins are also not rare. The Saoras even use wooden ear-ring.

Of the sixty-two tribal communities in Orissa, at least seven have significant mural paintings on the mud walls of their houses. The Saora wall paintings, which are popularly referred to as pictograms or icons have a ritual base. On the other hand, the wall paintings of the Juangs, the Bhuiyans, the Dongria Kondhs, the Santals, the Gadabas and the Gonds are more or less decorative in character and do not have any religious or ritual overtones.

Saora icon-making is related to primarily matters of health and disease, epidemics, death and child birth. There are two distinct stages in this plastic art. In the first stage the ritual divination by the priest leads to the identification of the 'spirit' or the 'power' that has caused a disease or death and that needs to be propitiated. It is at this stage that the words of the spell are used. Secondly, instead of an attempt to ward off the evil or malevolent spirit, here the spirit is brought in or rather pulled or dragged in and installed/imprisoned in a ritualistic, one-dimensional temple in the icon.

The spell also has two sequences. In the first part there is a general invocation to all gods and spirits that are supposed to inhabit the Saora world. In the second part the particular spirit is invoked to come and occupy the house that has been specially built for it.

After the incantation has been recited and the drawing or the icon, either by the Priest or the head of the household is more or less complete, the artist makes a salutation to the god or spirit by touching the ground with his head and then recites the following before giving final touches to the icon:

> "I have made a house for you. Here are your elephants, your horses. Come riding on them. Here are your suns and moons, crops and trees. Come and see what a nice house I have build for you with my own hands. Gods of the sky, come and see the house. Deities of the hills, come and see the house."

The Saora icons are drawn for the following purposes:

(1) Generally satisfying the deities and ancestral spirits,
(2) Averting any mishap including illness in the family,
(3) Reaping a bumber crop and improving the fertility of the soil,
(4) Enabling easy delivery of child.

The Saora houses are tiny structures with mud walls and thatched roofs. Very rarely, when a man is somewhat rich, the roof is of tiles. Sometimes it is also the dried palm leaves. The mud walls are generally smooth though not as elegant or even as smooth and firm as the mud walls of Santal houses. The icons are drawn on the inner side of the walls of a house. The major icon is drawn on the wall close to the entrance of the house or on the wall facing the front door. Sometimes in some houses smaller icons are also drawn on other walls of the house. These smaller icons are invariably drawn in places which do not come up to the eye sight as easily as those drawn near the front door. The Saora pictograms are curious amalgam of the traditional and the new. It is the product of an agricultural community in their emphasis on the sun, the acts of ploughing, broadcasting seeds, trees etc. And yet one also notices bicycles, automobiles, chairs and tables, confabulations and constructions—all the influence of the outside world impinging on their lives.

Unlike the Saora pictograms, the paintings and designs of the Santals, the Bhuiyans, the Dongria Kondhs, the Juangs, the Gonds and the Gadaba tribes are decorative in nature and purpose and do not have any religious-ritual basis. They flow out of the instinct to adorn and beautify one's house, the primary unit in which the individual and the family live their lives.

The walls of these types of houses generally provide the medium for washing with colour and sketching and painting a large variety of designs. These consist mostly of flowers, trees, creepers, birds and animals. Then there are the geometric designs. On the later a general remark may be made here. The Dongrias are very fond of triangular designs—a design which is found very liberally on the small scarf which they themselves weave on small looms. These triangular designs are very colourful and impressive. The Gadabas on the other hand are fond of squares and rectangles. These two groups rarely use circles or other complex geometrical patterns like hexagonals, hearts or aces.

The colour of reddish earth provides the background of the walls which is used as canvas. The pasted clay is smeared and allowed to dry up. The Santals tend to extend the frontiers of the imagination by drawing a cow eager to feed her calf; a peacock on a tree and an elephant on the ground almost seeking to touch each other; swans gliding past in water; elephants standing face to face with their trunks joined to each other; and almost a baffling variety of trees, flowering creepers and flowers in various stages of blooming. One does not notice any attempt at surrealistic presentation as in Saora pictograms. Here the attempt is at realism and depiction of known reality. The houses of the Santals indeed look very colourful because instead of patches of colour or paintings sometimes their entire wall-faces are colour-washed.

The Santals use mostly coloured earth for painting the walls of their houses. They are very lucky in this regard. For in the local area three colours which they prize for this purpose—white earth, red earth and yellow earth—are generally available. People dig up and collect earth of these colours and bring them to their houses for purposes of giving colour wash to the wall. The fourth primary colour which they use is black. Since no earth of this colour is available, they prepare it from indigenous materials. The wall paintings of the other tribal groups are merely variations on Santal wall paintings.

# 3 Art and the Primacy of the Person

THROUGHOUT history man has always looked upon art as one of his seminal defences against the erosion of time, against human fate. Not merely because it seeks to impose an order against the seeming chaos that is life and its flux; but also because it offers some consolation of continuity in the backdrop of the fleeting character of human existence. The dream has been: my words, my canvas, my song lives on even when I am no more. And others participate in the joys and sorrows of my words, of the colours in my canvas and the notes in my music or the rhythms in the dance.

Some even believe that the artist is engaged in a culpable rivalry with God, that he feels this world is a poor sketch of God, the artist and it deserves to be redone. Some believe no true artist ever tolerates reality, that his dream is to fashion an alternative universe in consonance with his dream.

It is from this, the role of the artist as he envisages it and as society looks upon it, emerges the key question of art's relationship to spirituality. Spirituality is a much misunderstood word in our times. Its detractors are many. But it is primarily a question of values, and approach. Spirituality is not a matter of religions, their dogmas, rituals or litanies. It is not a set of prescriptive canons of behaviour. It is not a rejection of a few things or acceptance of others. It is not sectarianism, God-men and their teachings. It is not also the story of superior Gods or lesser known God and God-men.

It is, on the contrary, the essence of our humanness, of our being human here and now, in this little planet that belongs to us all. It is not the story of a coming millennium or of a messiah who will come and deliver us from our *Karma*, our destiny. If we believe in such a deliverer, we may have to wait a long long time, could be till eternity. It may be a waiting for the Godot.

Human history is, on one hand, a record of madness, self-destruction and chaos. On the other, it is also a story of renewals, of new hopes and dreams, notwithstanding the soothsayers of doomsday. It is an assertion that man is greater than his history and that we have to be obsessed with the harvest and indifferent to history as the French poet Rene Char once said. And true spirituality lies in this: the assertion that every man carries a mystery within him and even when we may never know each other completely, we will need the whole of this life and may be many more lives to understand even a fraction of that mystery within myself and within you. It is an assertion that as a person you possess that beauty and value which is the most treasured thing on this planet. It is an assertion that just as I seek, in the little span of time that is allotted to me, the meaning of why I am here, I would protect, hold an open space for you so that you too can, in your own way, try to seek out that meaning.

Spirituality is not a dead shell of a form, a formula of prayer or litany. In our times its focus has to be on the primacy of the person. At its core a determined desire to live and let live, a feelling, as Albert Schweitzer used to say, "that I am life wishing to live in the midst of the lives that wish to live". It is also a undying faith in the terrible and beautiful grandeur of this planet and a unwillingness to treat it as a mere possession to be used or misused anyway we like. In short the essence of spirituality in our times is a reverence for life—a philosophy that is at the core of all religion and metaphysical thought but which gets lost in learned, arid and academic debates and institutional religions' organizational quarrels, their push and pull. And in our times nothing is more manifest than the poverty of the soul, the anomie of the heart, the loss of the capacity to believe in the celebration of life, its triumphs and tragedies, its ineluctable grandeur and its mellowed sorrows. There has been talk of a cancer in the soul, of the need for a human renewal, of the dehumanisation and vulgarisation of art. And at its heart is the dying ability to live experience, to rejoice in it, to see that each day is a new day, each sunrise and sunset yet another opportunity to savour life. Information, second hand information, often kills instinct. The individual ceases to feel, to imagine and permits others, the persuaders both hidden and not so hidden, to take over that role. Art's spiritual quest is to kindle the imagination to assert that each one of us has to perceive experience in our own way.

Art is thus in its essence a mode of expression of the human spirit, its essential humanness. Art and spirituality viewed in this broad sense are close allies of each other. They have the same basic origin in the fountain of life. They resist the forces of death and darkness, of barbarism and decay. They look towards a ceaseless quest for meaning and relevance, of renewal and regeneration. They can work together to assert once more what Blake asserted: "Everything that lives, lives not alone, nor for itself."

Our classical art traditions emphasised this essential dimension of art. Art was created for life and its fulfilment. Art was integral to life. It offered wisdom; it also offered happiness or pleasure. But it was a pleasure that lifted up the spirit and did not drag it towards mud and mire. Every individual was expected to participate in its grandeur if not as a creator, at least as a participative observer. This continued in the classical folk module for centuries. The folk forms of art—plastic, performing and literary also celebrated life; and man in society participated in it. Classical art developed first in the temples, in the places of worship and then traversed to men in society through royal courts but it kept up its search for excellence and its basic assertion of life and spirituality. Folk-art celebrated life in an even more intimate manner. Here the celebration of life was authentic and participative. Life and dream were welded together. The pleasure of participation was vital. And men sang and danced as they performed the ordinary jobs of life: hunting, sowing, reaping the harvest, worshipping Gods, celebrating the birth of a child, a marriage or bemoaning a death. Everything was a thanks-giving to the powers that be, for the fact of being alive. Words, gestures and rituals were fused in the primitive and folk dance-forms as much as in the classical ones. But then came the economic gate-keepers to art; all the media managers, the gallery and theatre owners, the critics, who not only take on the responsibility of promoting, defining and delineating art forms but also look upon art as yet another commodity to be sold in the market. It has a clientele, a target-group. It must cater to that group; it must find new consumers. Market research with a view to giving it a market orientation then slowly takes precedence.

It is no one's point that art should not reach out to masses. May be classical art went half-way towards this even as it emphasised its basic philosophy of excellence, of dedication and not popularity. Folk-art, because of its source and spread-effect had a much better access to the common man. But in neither art was looked upon as only another object to be bought for consumption. It was not a subject for seemingly intelligent, dilettante conversations in drawing rooms. Murals and paintings were not primarily for hotel lobbies or drawing rooms of the *nouveau rich*. It could be argued that murals were also done in temples, for religious purposes and sometimes at the behest of kings and priests. It could be said that the Maharis, the originators of the present Odissi dance, first danced for the Gods and then for the nobility. But art had not faced the multi-pronged pressures of a mass-market which is only another name for mass culture. In trying to cater to a commercially profitable market, art can lose its essential integrity and authenticity. It can throw up, duly sponsored and promoted by the media-managers and the economic gate-keepers, fake artists who do not hesitate to vulgarise or popularise it for their earnings. The market demand-supply formula takes over and art suffers in the process by lack of genuine development and loss of authenticity and purity. It no longer remains intimately linked to its spiritual roots—of seeking meaning of life and death, of asserting the primacy of the person, of being true to oneself—but to sell and sell more.

On the other hand, faced with such vulgarisation, genuine artists also tend to react by a withdrawal from the masses and thereby create some kind of a priestly class, a closed brotherhood that often seems oblivious of the people, the common man. Genuine art can suffer either way. By vulgarisation and commercialisation, by the urge only to sell reducing art to a commodity, and on the other hand, by the artists totally ignoring the masses from whose joys and sorrows and its intense realisation they derive strength and solidity for art. The landscape of art is a peopled landscape and not a hermetically sealed monad-like landscape with no human beings. On the other hand it is also a landscape meditating on itself, the artist constantly seeking, through himself and the 'other' in society, our ultimate meaning for being here on this earth. Art that negates its spiritual roots in this imaginative sense tends to become a mere object, a commodity. Art that forgets man and his world becomes a form of dilettantism and can at best become a product of an exclusive priestly class meant only for itself. Both can damage true art-creation and its linkage to true spirituality. Towards the human destiny of pain there are two approaches which can offer quite a bit of the much-needed consolation. They are the religious and the artistic. The former's role due to its chequered history has been rather non-uniform. Is it, therefore, too much to expect that art, in emphasising the urgency of human renewal, creates a new vision where ethics is transmitted into aesthetics?

# 4 Tradition in Modern Art

TRADITION is not merely the transmission or inheritance of things past. Only a few of the inherited or transmitted behaviour-patterns and value-systems can be considered as part of a given tradition and there is always an implication of a judgement about the value of the transmitted element.

A tradition is not merely a repetitive behavioural-pattern or some persistent symbol or motif in community culture. Behavioural and symbolic repetition through tradition is only an assertion of identity, a revival and regeneration of the life-force of the community. It is a song that raises echoes in the mind, links the past to the present through invisible bridges and often-leads to stability in the individual psyche and the social structure.

Tradition is often linked to religious motifs and ritual systems in the religious and even the secular order of values. Some of the essential characteristics of tradition are its indeterminacy and its ancient roots. The present and the future gain in strength, character and identity by emphasising certain desired traits. Each tradition incorporates in its fold a mythopoeic religious-ritual element which appeals to the subconscious of the community.

In the dynamics of culture-change, innovation has as important a place as continuity and tradition. As tradition implies a judgement about the value of certain socio-cultural mores in the transmitted element, the regard for tradition varies according to the degree of evolution of the society and its sense of cultural identity or self-image. Small and isolated pre-literate cultures possess an intense and compact oral tradition which governs most aspects of social behaviour as well as art creations. The artist in a primitive society is submerged in a creative continuum with the tradition. Innovation is only marginal and there is no serious break with the past or its traditions. There are no verbal or non-verbal stratagems that totally disrupt the link with tradition. The transformation of oral traditions into sophisticated academic traditions, the co-existence of a Great Tradition as well as of several interspersed, inter-woven small traditions and the emergence of mass culture as opposed to folk culture are some of the factors which complicate the relationship of the artist to his tradition.

Tradition implies a value judgement about the desirability or superiority of certain transmitted elements from the past. Often it has a religious-ritual aspect indicating the "delivering of precise deposit whose source is held to be divine to a specially selected person or persons". Thus an indeterminate and relatively ancient source from which the cultural matrix flows is favourable to a creation of tradition. More often than not it becomes a flattering self-portrayal of the past and helps maintain the cultural self-image of the community. This mythopoeic element, which enables a recreation or restatement of historical events so that they appear to be instances of the particular values or beliefs of the community has a special relevance in its relation to the artist. Tradition thus incorporates an exalted group consciousness which is enshrined in the belief of the community. Its primary characteristics of vagueness, remoteness of source and the wide network of ramifications make it the strong but invisible cementing force of the cultural matrix. A point of particular importance for the artist is whether a tradition is vital or has faded from race-memory and can only be evoked academically. Eliot's use of Tiresias in 'The Waste Land' is an example of the latter. Kazantzakis' use of the myth of Ulysses as a symbol of modern man may be another example.

It is possible that Eliot found no worthy follower precisely because of this: he was harking back to a tradition that was no longer part of the living tradition. It is a different story when an Indian author uses Duryodhana, Kubja, Jara the hunter or Yajati as diverse symbols for man and his predicament, the nemesis of conceit, the awakening to life, helplessness before the divine mystery or the unending quest for youth and vitality.

These mythological characters are part of the living tradition and folklore uses them in various contexts and as symbols. Thus they have an immediacy and relevance to today's existential context and can help solve the problem of communication. One can similarly see the tribal Santhal motif or the traditional patta painting recreated anew in a Jamini Roy.

No culture can be completely devoid of tradition though the intensity with which an artist is influenced by tradition may vary depending on the socio-cultural situation. If he is a prisoner of tradition, he can only be a purveyor of decadence. Tagore, who had perhaps a more acute sense of Indian tradition than many other artists and writers put it aptly when he said: "When in the name of Indian art we cultivate with deliberate aggressiveness a certain bigotry born of the habit of a past generation, we smother our soul under idiosyncracies unearthed from buried centuries. These are like masks with exaggerated grimaces that fail to respond to the ever-changing play of life".

And again: "All traditional structures of art must have a sufficient degree of elasticity to allow it to respond to varied impulses of life, delicate or virile: to grow with its growth, to dance with its rhythm. There are traditions which in alliance with rigid prescriptions of rhetoric establish their slave dynasty dethroning their master, the life-urge that revels in endless freedom of expression".

Tradition however involves, as Eliot reminded us, a perception not only of the pastness of the past but of its presentness. The sense of tradition was perhaps over-emphasized by Eliot when he considered it indispensable to anyone who would continue to be a poet beyond his twenty-fifth year. This again might be due to the search for the still centre, the moorings, the craving to return to roots which characterized a generation reeling under war and the depression. It was essentially a reaction to the outbreak of the irrational and the outpourings of the dark forces of disorder.

The sense of tradition involves an awareness of the contemporaneity of tradition and the traditionality of the present. This raises the important question of the nature of the creative process and the relation of the artist to society. The creative process is essentially a strange combination of the abilities to inherit tradition unobtrusively and extend its frontiers through the formation of new combinations of experience. If we believe that all art extols and denies at the same time and that it is engaged in a 'culpable rivalry with God' the significance of Rimbaud's 'derangement of the senses' and its opposite viewpoint namely, Eliot's 'escape from personality' become meaningful. In introducing Mexican poetry Octavio Paz observed 'poetry leaps into the unknown or it is nothing'. He could have said the same thing about all the arts. This leap into the unknown is derived from what he characterizes as its 'ancient subversive powers impregnated with eroticism and the occult'. This is precisely what primitive cultures emphasize as the essence of the creative process.

Participative, face-to-face culture makes possible a degree of sharing in art-creation and art enjoyment which is unthinkable in a more sophisticated and urbanized setting. In a changed setting, with growing materialism and an overriding emphasis on reason, the artist came to realize that intuition and the life of the imagination were at a low ebb and genuine creativity in the arts was a casualty.

This role of the artist has been emphasized in our times primarily due to the emergence or mass-society which is often the negation of the instinct of workmanship and the genuine creative process. Faced with the dehumanization of the arts, the artist believes that he has a special role in preserving art from an all-conquering materialism and vulgarity. The relationship between art and mass-society has thus brought into new focus the controversy between tradition and innovation in the arts. Eliot spoke of the progress of an artist as a continual self-sacrifice, a continual extinction of personality. To him no poet, no artist has his complete meaning alone. He emphasized that the mind of a mature poet or artist is a finely perfected medium in which very varied feelings are at liberty to enter into new combinations. It is this capacity for the fusion or fabricating of new combinations out of the given facts of everyday life that was to Eliot the most important aspect of the creative process.

The *avant-garde* artist, on the other hand, often accuses modern society of killing him, and Antonin Artaud in his biography of Van Gogh described the Dutch artist as a 'suicide of society'. The relationship between art and contemporary society was perhaps best expressed by Mallarmé when, borrowing a political image, he declared that in a period and culture like ours the artist finds himself 'on strike against society'. *Avant-garde* art is a minority culture which attacks and denies the majority culture of mass production, mass media and mass education. Forced to turn its back on society and tradition, it prefers to live in the desert of the isolated self on the mountain-top of its own solitude. He seeks to find consolation in his heroic destiny, in what Baudelaire called, his curse. In Nietzsche's terms, the artist believes that this fatal and prophetic element could be sublimated into a superior human creative activity that symbolized spiritual and mental health. The assertion of this quasi-religious vocation of the arts and the satanic impulse of revolt crystallized in Baudelaire's dictum, 'the man of letters is the enemy of the world' characterized a period of crisis in culture in which the artist has been conceived as a sort of sacrificial lamb, an innocent creature on whom society vents its own sense of guilt. His role may be compared to that of the Indian God of Destruction, Shiva, who as Nilakantha drank the poison that was destroying the world.

The emergence of mass culture has thus given a new currency to Rimbaud's idea of the derangement of the senses and a supposed identity between art and neurosis. All forms of alienation are basically pathetic and tragic. Rarely do they possess a heroic content. Tradition has also come to symbolize by some curious reasoning, the old world of faded colours and the values of kindness, mildness and decency as opposed to feelings of passion and revolt which characterize the modern temper.

One of the most ancient and persistent images in Western art is a lion devouring a horse or a deer. This became a decoration for Pagan sarcophagi and later entered the Christian iconography as a symbol of spiritual life. It finally became a dominating motif in the great religious painter of the nineteenth century, Delacroix. Kenneth Clerk quotes the answer to this puzzle in the words of a great living painter: "it is not enough to have the eyes of a gazelle: you also need the claws of a cat in order to capture your bird live and play with it before you eat and so join its life to yours". Perhaps the same answer was given in Blake's 'Marriage of Heaven and Hell'. Art thus depends on a condition of spiritual energy which must devour and transform all that is sluggish and phlegmatic in life.

In a society where art has to appeal to a mass audience the artist encounters a variety of economic gate-keepers: the impressarios, the promoters, the salesmen, the advertisers, the critics, etc. who often impose erroneous stereotypes of the public on the artist. As a reaction novelty in technique and rejection of anything traditional may become ends in themselves. As a result the artist's life-patterns are separated from the rest of society and aesthetic concerns only reflect and identify this separation. No work of art can be regarded simply as a dream. It is also a communication, a choice of gestures, verbal or non-verbal for introducing corresponding attitudes and empathy on the part of the audience.

We begin with the incantatory elements in art the conception of art as a prayer, as a ritual offering in the hands of a shaman or a priest who knows the rules of the game, a game that many have to play together in the brief interlude between life and death, in ecstasy and in pain, in jubilant celebration and in lonely grief. This is why even while art is to be looked upon as being an exploration of the unknown and therefore primarily innonative, one cannot completely do away with the role of tradition and its emphasis on the continuity of the cultural self-image of the group. In all traditional societies where art is a part of the general life of the people, in all primitive societies, there is no real distinction between art and life or the fine arts and the applied arts. The separation of art and life, action and dream which characterize mass societies today, was never true of ancient societies. Yet with the differentiation of the applied arts from fine arts and the latter becoming the special intellectual occupation of a sophisticated elite, the existence of tradition presents difficulties. The more specialized the artistic segment of the community the greater is the urge to deny tradition and society and to extol only the devilish dark energy of the creative self which Lorca characterized as *duende*.

Some of the finest creative works of the last two centuries have emerged from such an emphasis on the dark energy of creativity, a secret fiesta as Octavio Paz puts it. Faced with the

vulgarity of mass culture, the artist seems to have adopted this peculiar form of bigotry.

Art stands the risk of a total alienation from the life of the community and there is a need to emphasize the relevance of tradition to the contemporary milieu and to marry the temporal and the timeless.

After all art is a curious alchemy. In the words of St. John Perse, "it is action, it is passion, it is power and always the innovation that extends borders. Love is its hearth-fire: insurrection its law; its place is everywhere in anticipation; it wants neither to deny nor to keep aloof. It expects no benefits from the advantages of its time. Attached to its own destiny and free from any ideology it clasps both past and future in the present, the human with the super-human".

# 5 Shakespeare, or a Pair of Shoes? Art and the Market

WHAT indeed is an object of art and what is its essence? What is it that distinguishes it from numerous other objects found in nature created, fabricated, made and manufactured by human imagination, ingenuity and skill? Is there something a little extra, perhaps a touch of the dark energy or vision of the artist, the *duende* of which Lorca spoke, which lifts the ordinary clay or metal, timber or canvas to the level of art and distinguishes an art object from other objects?

There have been various answers to these fundamental questions through man's chequred history. If art is the expression of the instinct of workmanship in every man and the extension of the artist's personality, it is also the product of imagination, a symbol or an idea taking shape in the dark womb of the artist's psyche. If it is a vision, a dream, it is also a product of his hands, a craft, using objects like brush and paint, paper and mud wall which have a cost. It is action, symbolic action. It is also the dream, the unending dream which the ancient caveman-hunter tried to ritually materialise on cave walls so that he would have better luck with the hunted animal. It is the dream which a Picasso and an old woman painter of Madhubani, an Amrita Shergil and a poor patta painter of Orissa's coastal village Raghurajpur have in common.

Often our dreams and our actions are considered to be mutually exclusive, divergent and even hostile to each other. It is held that there is a time for action and there is a time for dreaming. Further the logic is carried to social strata and economic classifications. It is held that the leisured class can create art, can enjoy it. The ordinary man cares more for bread and less for the moon.

It is the old question of the plays of Shakespeare or a pair of shoes. But human history has shown that in ancient societies men created art as they worked. Art was an integral part of life. It was not the concern of a small elite which, in our times, is progressively turning itself into an exclusive brotherhood.

Art was created in the open world of social action. Men created art as they built their houses, sang, danced, painted their mud walls and hill faces, carved out forms from formless stones, worshipped the unseen powers. Together, in groups, in ecstasy and in anguish, to celebrate and to commemorate. And Marx had the vision that the artist tomorrow would bridge the gap between action and dream. Yet to do that and thereby to render unnecessary the economic gate-keepers to art, the professional critic, the gallery managers, the media advertisers, all those hidden persuaders who form our opinion and views on various art creations.

This is not to deny the value of the personal dream in art nor to underestimate the anguish of the artist engaged in the task of giving his dream a local habitation and a name. Nor can one wish away all the economic gate-keepers in the art world today. This is only to say that basically art is the creation of what Huizinga in his *Decline of the Middle Ages* called the *home ludens*, of man the player.

In all art there is an element of play; to play with objects, forms, colours, sounds, words; to play with dreams and visions, tragedies and triumphs, loves and deaths. Art connects, it does not alienate or isolate. Art brings us back to our most ancient dreams, our still-remembered sorrows and hopes. It is, as Andre Malraux once said, 'one of our fundamental defences against destiny'. In popular art, to a large extent, action and dreams merge. Often we forget that if an art is popular it is not necessarily inferior. Nor that the less popular a piece of art, the greater its intrinsic value.

If a piece of art is symbolic action, the meeting ground of action and dream, it is also a physical object, a commodity. As a commodity it has a value, an assigned value. A value determined not merely by its aesthetic charm and grace but also, more mundanely, in terms of its market costs, its economics. How much money has gone into its making. No doubt, value here is highly relative, linked as it is to the level of appreciation of the community and the prevailing value-system in general. A patta painting, a Madhubani painting may be needed for five-star hotel foyers; folk-art objects may become an inevitable necessity in drawing rooms of the *nouveau riche*. And paintings are auctioned.

Art as commodity only pre-supposes a value attached to it. It also pre-supposes a fairly developed monetised market and a market-orientation. It also pre-supposes a technological orientation, recource to aids that could render multiplication of art objects possible for the clientele. Multiplication and reproduction become important. Art tends to be looked upon also as a product, a commodity not merely to be seen or admired in a temple, or a gallery or museum but to be owned, purchased.

In India popular art objects had been bought and sold in the 18th and 19th centuries and even earlier. Around religious centres like Nathdwara in Rajasthan, Kalighat in Calcutta and Puri in Orissa, individual styles of paintings had developed, catering to the needs of the local people. Art had a religious overtone, a ritualistic purpose both in the inspiration to create and the motivation to own. The visiting pilgrims craved to own it for religious purposes and the creators of the art objects made a decent living through selling them. It was called 'bazar art' not in its current pejorative sense.

The evolution of the printing press in India in Serampore in the 18th century gave a big boost to reproduction of art objects. Lithographs reached India in the first quarter of the 19th century and later, in 1860 A.D., chromolithographs with shiny, greyish products started appealing to the popular market. Wood engravings, metal etchings, lithographs and allied technologies led to mass production of cheap pictures; of gods, goddesses, landscapes, of nature and social events. Indigo stuff packing, woodblock prints, bidi labels, cheaper calendars and so on, slowly began to dominate, and paintings at the pilgrim centres changed in style and production patterns to cater to the evolving market conditions.

Popular art does not base itself on the desideratum of art *merely* as a commodity. To the extent it does, it is honest and forthright and serves the objective of art and the artistic community. Sophisticated, high-level art, on the other hand, can and frequently does treat art objects as commodities whose possession is itself not merely a status symol or a passport to culture but also a mechanism of patronising the arts.

Thereby it often caters to the machinations and whims of the various hidden persuaders and economic gate-keepers who guard the fortress of high art. In the process objects of art sometimes tend to become *merely commodities* and run the risk of generating false and distorted value systems and cultural patterns. They also tend to create a wall between the artists and the community in which they work by choking or denying the social origins of art and its aesthetic dimensions. They tend to make art the prerogative of only a privileged few, which can resemble a priesthood in its isolation and exclusiveness.

Art is no doubt, to an extent, a commodity. It has a value. A value in terms of its technological orientation and its market orientation. The mode of production or reproduction of an art piece does determine its economic cost. The raw materials, the ingredients that go into its making or its duplication and the labour of the artist are extremely difficult to determine for they would often depend on the artist's assigned status and his popularity in the market. The latter is a part of marketing orientation, something answering to the law of supply and demand.

In India, however, at least till recently there was never any attempt to distinguish art from craft. In fact *shilpa* variously meant art, skill, design, architecture and also craft. This is why the general conception of art was a much broader one and never applied to the private studio of an individual artist. It did treat art as commodity but the motivation was to reach out to a large clientele at a very reasonable price consistent with the cost of production.

# 6 Oral Tradition: Words, Signs and Gestures

HISTORIANS of culture have discussed at length the dichotomies and binary opposition between 'oral or preliterate culture' and 'literate culture'; between 'oral tradition' and 'written tradition'. Among oral cultures there have been, and continue to be, the primary oral cultures where there is no knowledge whatsoever of writing, where the word uttered is simply a sound carried from a speaker to the listener or listeners. There were also for a long-time in history, until at least the emergence of printing technology, other oral cultures which depended on the text written by hand; the text that could be written out again either by the same person or copied by another. Ideas on culture in our times have been so deeply influenced by the use of writing, literacy, written texts, and the electronic media that it has become nearly impossible to realise that the literate culture, historically speaking, occupies only a small fragment of man's long cultural history. And understanding the nature of this oral tradition and the orality of culture has become, because of the dogmas and theories we have got used to, as difficult as understanding camels if we are told that they are automobiles without wheels, assuming a population which has never seen a camel.

In highlighting orality-literacy contrasts and relationships W.J. Ong[1] has done a signal service to the understanding of the several interlocking aspects of our human condition and the need for approaching orality and literacy both synchronically—comparing oral cultures and chirographic cultures coexisting at a given period of time—and also diachronically. In a very real sense in the beginning was the word, the spoken word—and society came into being with oral speech. We became literate very late in history.

If the history of the *homo sapien* goes back approximately fifty thousand years into the past, the earliest script is not more than six thousand years. We have passed from the stage of pristine or pure oral culture to the written or chirographic culture, then to print or typographic culture and now the electronic culture that makes use of both writing and print as its foundation.

If the Vedas or the Illiad were the flowerings of *Sruti* or oral culture, surely it is necessary to go back in time to them and even beyond them to understand our today and its electronic culture as well as the role of verbalisation in managing our knowledge of the world and about ourselves. For the function of verbalisation as much as of print or of the electronic media, is to infuse meaning into the apparent meaninglessness of time and its flux and to impose an order on the apparent chaos of the movement of events, which is yet another dimension of time.

Oral tradition is structured on orality but orality itself is a loaded and fairly ambiguous term. It is all the more problematic when we have to analyse it as a functional dimension of a written text which, after all, was its function for a long long time and which is still its function in many oral cultures round the globe.

We may, however, first look into the basic difference between oral and written verbalisation both as activities of the mind and from the point of view of their social dimensions.

The utterance of a word is a sound and the word becomes a 'winged' sound. Basically it is meant for the other listener, the others out there; but to an extent the speaker also partakes of it. In fact this later function, some socio-linguists assert, is also a basic function of oral speech. It is thus a participatory activity: the source, the repository of knowledge, idea or information is communicating to others; in the process it cannot only erase or modify what it says in one breath but also can get a reply or response from the other side. It is thus situated in an ingrained participative face-to-face universe. This holds good not only of the oral tradition still prevalent in India, its still largely illiterate rural and tribal population but also in large parts of the Third World and also in Euro-American societies in a limited way. Even where it is not a primary oral culture completely ignorant of writing, orality still enioys a valued place.

Orality and oral tradition rest on communitarian togetherness and the emphasis on the sacral. The Hebrew *dabar*, which means word, means also event and thus directly refers to the spoken word. As Ong would say, "the spoken word is always an event, a movement in time, completely lacking in the thing-like repose of the written or printed word".[2] The spoken word thus interweaves and integrates human beings into close-knit units, groups and brotherhoods.

Writing and print, on the other hand, isolate. Readership is, after all, an abstraction, an aggregation in a statistical frame. By contrast the audience for oral tradition is a concrete, palpable reality and the oral utterance has an interiorising force which is denied to the written or printed word staring out from a page at the reader. Besides this the oral word and the tradition it builds is intimately linked to ultimate questions of life and death, the intricate questions of existence and is thus linked to the world of faith and belief, in short, the sacral world.

In all primary oral cultures and in most literate oral cultures the sacral heavily depends on the utterance of the word. The village-priest in most primitive societies has to recite, invoke, read aloud the enchanted words, the mantras, the holy utterances. It is an incantation. The world over, from American Indian incantions to Dongria Kondhs' Meria Sloka, from Bushmen's invocations to Santal *bakhens*, the strength of the sacral utterance is in the sound. Even in Christianity the Bible is required to be read aloud in liturgical services. God, after all, always *speaks* to human beings and never *writes* a letter to anyone. God the father 'speaks' his Son: he does not inscribe him. Jesus, the Word of God, left nothing in writing though he could read and write (Luke 4:16). The letter kills, the spirit (breath, on which rides the spokene word) gives life (2 corinthians 3: 6).

In the act of writing the universe is, by contrast, a completely lonely world. The writer as he plants word after word on the blank landscape of the paper or takes it out on the typewriter, is lonely, utterly lonely. Creative writers have spoken of the awesome loneliness of the business of writing. And the act is directed, even when admittedly it could be partially for self-realisation—at absent, contingent readers whom the writer does not even know. They could be those now living, may be in different cultures and different countries, they could also be those yet to be born. This is so unlike the destiny of the speaker in a primarily oral culture. Then again the reader is also submerged in a loneliness as he reads. There is no possibility of a concrete dialogue, the author is not present before him; it is only his blank words staring out from the page. There is thus not even the possibility of a participative, communitarian universe emerging out of it. The world of difference between oral traditions and oral cultures on one hand and the literate, written culture on the other is largely relatable to the functional modes of sight and sound. While sight *isolates* by posting the viewer and the object viewed at two different areas of space, sound can submerge, can integrate, for it pours into the listener from all directions of space.

Merlau-Ponty[3] very rightly observes that vision *dissects* for it is bound by specific direction and one can see another thing, not before it, only by lifting away one's eyes from it. The auditory activity is thus integrating, unifying and not isolating. And if we remember that at the heart of knowledge there is the grand principle, not of fractioning or dissection but of unification, integration and harmonisation, then we are not far from realising the great civilisational role of oral tradition and oral cultures.

Thus oral traditions, primary oral cultures, have not only characterised the larger part of the history of *homo sapiens* on this planet but have also been the repository of knowledge, ideas, cultural traits and informations including that most vital aspect of human growth in ancient civilization, namely the sacral. The kind of literacy that has been developed in the West since Industrial Revolution tends to obscure the basic facts regarding the original and basic orality of reading. In the long march of modern culture and more specifically the modern Western culture that dominates it, it is easy to forget that the "oral uses of language, including the language of the written word, have been not only present but dominant for much of the more than two-and-one-half millenia since the development of alphabetic writing among the Greeks".[4]

## II

There has been debate as to the precise historical point in time which marks the transition from primarily oral culture and tradition to primarily literate book culture. The Greek bias against the written word is well-known. It is comparable to the bias against computer in its early days or against children's use of calculator from parents. The ground is the same, the much-quoted diatribe of Socrates as recorded in Plato's *Phaedrus*[5]: that it undermines memory by seeking to posit outside the mind what intrinsically belongs to it and, therefore, should only be there. We read of a report that of the Athenians taken prisoner at Syracuse in 413, those who could recite Euripides for their captors were able to gain their release. This would gladden the hearts of the singers of the four-hour long Binti songs in a Santal marriage to discover their ancestry.

Aristotle is often taken to represent the transition from oral tradition to written culture. But even in medieval Europe the more important thing, even when manuscripts could be copied, was its memorising and reading aloud and this was no different from what had been and in many respects continues to be, the oral traditions in Hindu, Muslim, Buddhist and other cultures in matters both sacral and non-sacral. In most of the Third World the oral tradition is so strong and so deeply entrenched that it is even today not merely the carrier and the most useful mode of socialisation both in religious matters and matters of faith and also in all day-to-day matters of social mores, lore of the tribe, cosmogony, customs, economic activities etc.

Even in the West hearing of the scriptures was often a stimulus to acquire the ability to read and perform the sacred but social function of reading it to others. Margaret Aston writes about books themselves becoming voice. "Wherever they existed they were heard as well as seen and the reverberations of vocalised texts resounded outwards."[6] On the other hand McLuhan has told us that "as the Gutenberg typography filled the world the human voice closed down. People began to read silently and passively as consumers".[7]

Thus even while recognising the historical contribution of oral traditions to human civilisation and its continuing role in human affairs it is necessary to recognise the need for proper documentation of the 'triumph of the silent page'. W. A. Graham quotes Adam Muller, a contemporary of Schiller who lamented that "once speech has been transposed most unnaturally from the domain of the ear to the domain of the reading eye, from the domain of the voice to the province of the writing hand, it then dries up more and more, and shrivels away: the word shrinks into itself and becomes more and more a cipher".[8]

Is reading then simply a mental cognition of visual symbols on a written page, "the mode or communication to a silent reader through the eye alone from a definitive written text", as Ruth Finnegan[9] would have us believe? Apparently it looks to be the truth. But there are also those who believe, like Ong (and also Saussure, Havelock and Lloyd James) that 'reading' a text means converting it to sound, aloud, subvocally, or in the imagination, syllable-by-syllable in slow reading or sketchily in the rapid reading common to high-technology cultures".[10] It may be possible to call to mind the picture of a silent listener to his own silent recitation. That would once again emphasise the seminal nature of oral sepeech as the foundation of oral tradition and the most intrinsic form of human communication. One 'mouthed' the words of the text and preferably voiced them aloud. This was common in Western Europe even in 19th century.

The oral tradition's strength is, however, not in the scriptural tradition though that may have been the original inspiration as well as the continuing and most pervasive concern. Graham in his *Beyond The Written Word* adapts the Indian paradigm to study scriptures as spoken word. He quotes Maurice Bloomfield approvingly of the Vedic tradition being in some respects the most remarkable in recorded history and from that period we have received, as he asserts, "not one single piece of antiquarian or archaeological material, not one bit of real property; not a building, nor a monument; not a coin, jewel or utensil;—nothing but winged words".[11] In fact other scholars have accepted the conceptualisation of the venture "as a typology of the Word rather than one of scripture, the Hindu life".[12] And he uses a vast repertoire of knowledge of non-vedic texts from *Ramayana* to *Ramacharita Manasa*, *Devi Mahatmya* and extends the validity of his assertion to Islam and Christian theologies.

III

As has been briefly mentioned earlier the range of oral tradition covers also the non-sacral world of knowledge and information and is the only pragmatic way of socialisation, learning and transmission of knowledge and information. The print textuality of modern culture should not, therefore, blind anyone to the historical and civilisational role of oral traditions.

Writing changes the fundamental modes of assimilating information and ideas that a culture generates. When memory cannot treasure in its archives temporality and its distinctiveness as well as 'pastness', the narrative loses its relevance. This is where oral myth differs from written narrative modes. It is not their relative truth that is at stake but their presentation of time and flux. The oral tradition does this in a synchronic frame, something akin to what Mircea Eliade calls 'time out of time' but the written narrative goes over to a diachronic linear sequencing of time which no doubt makes historical enquiry possible. The homeostatic process of forgetting or transforming myth or parts of a tradition which is available to an oral culture is no longer available to a written culture as it cannot discard, absorb or transmute the past in the same way.

Despite the already vast and growing literature in this area there is, however, need for further research to let us understand more meaningfully the contrast between oral cultures and chirographic cultures. For so far there has only been a comparison between orality and alphabetic writing. We can't afford to forget that there have also been other writing systems including the Mesopotamian Cuneiform, the Egyptian hieroglyphics, the Minoan Linear B, the Indus Valley Script as also the Chinese, the Mayan and the Aztec Scripts.

Writing no doubt is a solipsistic operation and words are alone in a text lacking full phonetic qualities. But are they signs and if so where after all do they point? The sign language does not necessarily have to be embodied in words; they could be in other symbols, other modes of pictograph or icon. Instead, in the primitive mind and in most primitive societies, the word was non-different from the object symbolised. The Santal *bakhen* would not name a snake for fear that it may then materialise. Instead it would refer to it as 'a small piece of polished rope'. Malinowski made that very important point that among primitive people with oral cultures the "word was itself a mode of action and not simply a countersign of thought".[13]

All sound which comes from within and so all oral utterances are basically dynamic. They are not oriented to knowledge or information. They are not primarily signs pointing to a mode of thought or a mode of perception or activising the mind that way. They are basically modes of action with varying degrees of magical potency. Often they are powered and are always assimilated to things. Not that words in oral tradition do not carry ideas or thoughts. These in fact can be a large variety of ideas or perceived notions differing in the way they carry them. Ong has sought to enumerate their variety. They have, according to him, the following qualities in organising thought but they are not signs:

(*a*) They are aggregative rather than analytic;
(*b*) either redundant or copious;
(*c*) conservative or traditionalist;
(*d*) additive rather than subordinative;
(*e*) close to the human life world;
(*f*) agnostically toned;
(*g*) empathetic and participatory rather than objectively distanced;
(*h*) situational rather than abstract; and
(*i*) above all, homeostatic.

It would not, therefore, be difficult to see why words in oral tradition cannot be basically signs. If anything they are more akin in gestures. Visions can register motion as well as stillness. But the orality of language or primary orality of speech based on sound cannot be picturised in immobility. The basic characteristic of sound which frames orality is movement. There is nothing comparable in sound to a still shot in the visual world. Orality, therefore, cannot work as sign. Words in oral culture do not, therefore, try to point to any signs. They are either action, materialisation of objects or variously-loaded gestures.

Jacques Derrida has made the same point very clearly in his monumental work *Of Grammatology* (1976). He holds that "there is no *lingusitic sign* before writing".[14] In other words the written word alone can or does behave as a sign. This is because thought builds its nest primarily in speech and not in texts, and texts derive their meanings through references of the visible symbol to the world of sound". After all 'sign' refers to something visually apprehended. Sign is derived from the Roman word *signum* which was the standard that a unit of Roman army carried aloft for visual identification. It was itself a pictorial design and not letters or words even though Romans themselves were literate.

There were iconographic symbols even as late as European Renaissance, Ivy bush, for example, meant a tavern and a pole meant a barber shop. I find an interesting parallel in what the late Pandit Raghunath Murmu told me in elaborate discussion in 1975 as to his resources in framing the 01 Chiki, the alphabet of the Santals. He said that he had taken these from the tattoo marks on cattle, the signs on boulders and stones which told the fellow tribals that 'this way there is danger', or that 'run away from here' etc.

'Our complacency', says Ong, "in thinking of words as signs is due to the tendency, perhaps incipient in oral cultures but clearly marked in chirographic cultures and far more marked in typographic and electronic cultures, to reduce all sensation and indeed all human experience to visual analogues".[16] Oral tradition uses words as sound and sound is a relentless march in time. Time can only be tamed spatially in clock and calendar but at its best it becomes only a falsification. For time arrested is not real time.

As regards words in oral tradition as gestures it is worthwhile remembering that in life when words fail to convey what we want—whether in oral or chirographic or electronic culture—we use gestures. Gesture, Kenneth Burke urges, is basically symbolic action and that corresponds more meaningfully to what has been said earlier about the context of words as sound in oral cultures and traditions and words symbolising action. The line in *Othello*, "I understand the fury in your words. But not the words", precisely brings out the quality and nature of gesture in primary oral cultures. Gesture dominates not only the word spoken in such cultures; it also dominates painting, sculpture, dance and music both in oral cultures and in modern written cultures. In Blackmur's words, "we feel almost everything that deeply stirs us as if it were a gesture, the gesture of our uncreated selves."[16] Oral cultures and oral traditions always had and continue to have a deeper and more sensual awareness of our uncreated selves and its symbolisation through gestures and therein lies their continued relevance.

## NOTES


1. Ong, W.J. (1982): *Orality and Literacy*: *The Technologizing of the Word*, London and New York, Methuen.
2. Ong, W.J.: Ibid, p. 75.
3. Merlau-Ponty, Maurice (1961): "L'oeil et l'espirit", *Les Temps Modernes* No. 18, p. 184.
4. Graham, W.A. (1987): *Beyond The Written Word*, Cambridge University Press, New York, p. 33.
5. Plato (1973): *Phaedrus and Leters VII and VIII* translated with introduction by Walter Hamilton; Penguin Books, England.
6. Aston, Margaret (1977): *Lollardy, and Literacy, History*-62, pp. 347-71.
7. McLuhan, M. (1962): *Gutenburg Galaxy*: *The Making of Typographic Man*, University of Toronto Press, Toronto, p. 250.
8. Graham, W.A.: Ibid, p. 44.
9. Finnegan, Ruth (1977): *Oral Poetry*, Cambridge University Press, USA, p. 29.
10. Ong, W.J.: Ibid p. 8.
11. Graham, W.A.: Ibid p. 67.
12. Coburn, Thomas B (1984): *Scripture in India*: *Towards a Typology of the Word in Hindu Life*, Journal of the American Academy of Religion, pp. 435-59.
13. Malinowski, B. (1923): *The Problem of Meaning in Primitive Languages*, in Odgen C.K. and Richards, I.A. (edited) *The Meaning of Meaning* New York, Harcourt Brace pp. 451 and 470-81.
14. Derrida, Jacques (1976): *Of Grammatology*, translated by Gayatṛi Chakravorty Spivak, Johns Hopkins University Press, Baltimore and London, p. 14.
15. Ong, W.J.: Ibid p. 76.
16. Blackmur, R.P. (1954): *Language As Gesture*: *Essays in Poetry*, Henderson and Spalding, London, p. 24.

# 7 Singing of Life: The World of India's Tribal Poetry

IT WAS A sparkling moon-lit night in a lonely tribal village of Orissa lost in the midst of dense forests: the night of full-moon in the month of *Pous* (corresponding to January) and one of the most imortant festivals of the Mundas. The lonely village street near the *Akhra* was gradually filling up with the villagers. In groups they came, boys and girls, old men and women, dressed for the dance, humming tunes in high spirits. It was no longer the same village I had seen in the daytime: featureless, squalid and ordinary. It had been transformed by the magic of moonlight and the exuberance of spirit all round. They danced and they sang. Ancient, timeless songs. Old as the neighbouring hills, ancient as the moon. There were sprinklings of improvisations, and interpolations, from the new world growing up around them; the world of development blocks, jeeps, village-level workers, of Government, fertilizers, insecticides and birth control pills. But these were mostly from the dancers of the younger generation. An old tribal sat by my side watching the dance, almost completely drunk, and looking very much lost. Suddenly he broke into song, like a winter tree coming into leaf. I can still hear the soft agony of that ageless voice and song. It was a part of that natural order, the lonely moon-lit night of the empty mountains and forests, almost the voice of the night. Then I knew the tragedy inherent in the situation; the near-impossibility of integrating the tribal people into the greater society while preserving intact their cultural antonomy and individuality. It was only right that public policy should not treat them merely as museum specimens to be preserved isolated and uncontaminated by modern society, in deep forests for study as 'noble savages' by the scholars from cities. But may not socio-economic integration for the tribes bring about a cultural anomie, a drying-up of those sources of fulness of spirit, dark energy and exuberance that characterise much of the tribal way of life? May not their own oral tradition of songs be either forgotten, despised or hybridised by treatment with 'insecticides' and 'pills', by their own younger generation? May not acculturation and growing sophistication kill the authenticity of life, art-form and songs of these simple tribals? May not the more educated young men reject the very social milieu of which these songs and dances are the symbols? Certainly these songs deserve to be collected and preserved before perhaps they are sung no more and, maybe, die out.

That was in 1968 when the author was Deputy Commissioner of Sundergarh district, a district in Northern Orissa where the Rourkela Steel Plant has come up in the heartland of the tribal region. More than fifty per cent of this district's population which adjoins South Bihar are tribals. I was fascinated by the cadence and wistfulness of the music inherent in the tribal songs which I heard, either in villages on special festival occasions or, while driving along the streets, from groups of tribal women, singing as they returned either from the agricultural field or from the mines. I wanted to look at the text of the songs. When I did, the density of their communicative images and the sheer simplicity and evocativeness of the lines touched me as a poet. I took two years to learn the Santali language with the help of my personal staff of the district and slowly acquired the capacity to be able to talk to them reasonably well. I realised how, as Sartre would say, language is our antena, our looking glasses. In fact for anyone working in tribal areas, on any aspect of tribal culture, knowledge of the relevant tribal language is essential. It is only then they open out to you. Even then you have to have infinite patience and never force the pace, for the tribals are not fond of hurry and they are not used to suspicious instruction into their affairs by others. What you need is infinite measure is the bird watcher's patience and deep love.

Since 1968 this has been a continuing passion for me. Slowly over the years I have worked in this tribal region of Eastern India, taken two years sabbatical on a prestigious Homi Bhabha Fellowship (1975-77) and translated into English, with critical introduction, nine anthologies of their oral poetry which have been extremely well received both in India and abroad. I have also felt that my learning of at least one major language namely, Santali has helped me a lot so that at least the other tribal languages which are analogous to it—and there are at least 4 such languages—have become accessible to me. This has helped me to be as near to the originals of the poems in my translation as possible.

Later, besides the nine anthologies of oral poetry edited by me, I have published four major works on the nature of transformation of tribal societies and their cultural traditions. They are:

(*i*) Modernisation and Ritual,
(*ii*) The Realm of the Sacred,
(*iii*) Tribal Wall Painting of Orissa, and
(*vi*) Tribal Life and Culture of Orissa.

It has thus been a matter of immense love and whenever there has been an opportunity I have gone back to these tribal regions to continue with my interest in their poetry and culture.

The primitive poem or song is part of a complex of communal activity, which includes singing, dancing, religious celebration and celebration of social occasions. The songs, the dances and the relevant festivities are intimately and integrally related. For celebrating each important religious festival or socio-religious ceremony, the tribals have an appropriate set of songs and dances. It is necessary to view these poem-songs as part of such a total communal activity, which is not true of modern poetry.

The recognised performers remember the songs very well, particularly when they happen to be of the older generation. Most of the songs circulate by the process of oral transmission and their roots lie buried deep in the group-life of the tribes. There are no fixed song-makers and no attempt is made to take credit for having discovered or improvised any song. Most of the songs have come down from generations and performers learn them from their elders. The continuity of the old tradition is thus maintained.

The poems or songs often accompany dancers. The recitation

of the words and the movement of the body are the two co-ordinates of the graph of socio-religious and ritual action which they define and describe. Curt Sachs, the noted authority on primitive dance, has said that, for the primitive, "dance was a means of control over the surroundings". This endeavours to gain control over nature expressed itself through a psychological process of sympathetic transcreation. And the transcreation was a combination of bodily gestures, verbal symbolism and prescribed ritual action. For example, the Sarhul festival of the Mundas is partly a vegetation ceremony and also partly a fecundity ceremony. The ceremonial bath, the stacking of rice in baskets and the offering of rice beer to the village ancestors and using some of this rice for sowing is associated with fertility. It is thus an invocation for more members in the tribe, for more sons and daughters. The Sarhul procession is taken out to the village sarna, the village deity. The festival is celebrated by liberal drinking and dancing. The pattern of dancing thus gets integrally related to the text and meaning of the song and the rituals accompanying it.

The anonymity of the song-makers is a notable phenomenon in primitive society. The absence of a written language makes the process of transmission of the songs with their complex structure of social and communal association an amazing phenomenon. For the arrangement of words, the stylistic pattern and the grouping of images remain virtually unchanged over the years and this is largely because of this unwritten, oral character. "Anonymity in the present structure of society", said Robert Graves, "usually implies that the author is ashamed of his authorship or afraid of the consequences if he reveals himself; but in a primitive society, it is due to just the carelessness about the author's name." This kind of carelessness is inherent in the primitive mind, for what is important for him is the song and not the song-maker. To that extent he can be compared to the unknown artists, painters and sculptors, who in Konark, in Khajuraho and all the world over, in sculpture, architecture and painting, have not left behind their names even while enriching the common heritage of humankind. The primitive mind does not know the emphasis on the ego, the 'conceit' of the author which the twentieth century has brought so much to the forefront. The lack of any personal aspiration and ambition for name and fame makes these songs so much more genuine and authentic. The songs remain; the emotions they convey remain for the creator's sons and daughters, and their offspring after them. What more could the primitive singer wish for himself!

The world of oral poetry of Indian primitive tribes is an almost unexplored but vanishing world. Archer, Elwin and perhaps a few other scholars have gathered and presented some of this vast body of poetry. But they have only touched the tip of the iceberg, Hundreds of thousands of songs remain undocumented. And what is more important, with rapid socio-economic transformation they run the risk of dying out or being distorted beyond recognition. There are a very large number of tribes. Even in respect of the three States in eastern India—Orissa, Bihar and West Bengal—there are nearly one hundred tribal groups. In Orissa alone there are sixtytwo groups. What is analysed here are only small selections from the poetry of seven selected tribes in these States.

Far too long have the songs, the tales, the mythologies, the rituals and legends of the 'primitive' tribes been treated as mere ethnological data; and, in an age of the assumed superiority of economic analysis of ethnographic materials, no wonder they are looked upon as somewhat residuary and unscientific and, in any case, of only marginal interest to the social anthropologist. This situation is not peculiar to India. It is a world-wide phenomenon. A time has come when it must be realised that, while we can speak of stages in technological growth, the same cannot be said of growth or efflorescence in the field of culture. There is no linear growth in the cultures of societies and all aspects of culture may not be susceptible to economic analysis. And the word 'primitive' itself is somewhat of a misnomer. The Aztecs, the Mayas were also perhaps 'primitives' from this point of view. Levels of culture are not proportionately related to either levels of economic affluence, personal incomes or levels of consumption or the capacity of the individual as a waste-maker. Social anthropology has to view these data as extremely significant tools of analysing personality traits, normative attitudes and social actions and behaviour-patterns. Scientism, whether of economic or political anthropology, can be a fallacy if not seen in the perspective of social processes, personal responses and inter-personal relationships. Further, it is high time we realised the immense value of these songs, legends, and mythologies, as literature *per se*. The absence of a written language, a script or proclaimed authorship of the songs or narrations do not in any way detract from the excellence of the songs or poems. All the song-poems are in fact anonymously authored. But, as Robert Graves stressed, contrary to the situation in modern societies anonymity is favoured not for avoiding guilt or embarrassment but because of the absence of a heightened ego which would claim any art-creation as that of the individual creator.

Years back Arthur Waley complained of the almost total lack of attention by the ethnologists to unwritten poetry. He observed, "Ethnological interest goes in waves. Now it is skulls, now it is kinship ties, now it is 'character-types'." So far songs have never been the fashion. It is easy enough to substantiate this assertion. For example, the most recent general work on primitive life, Boas's *General Anthropology* has only four or five pages on song, as opposed to a hundred pages on economic organization. Another proof of the lack of work upon traditional song is the fact that when in 1934 the Anthropological Congress was held in London, out of nearly a hundred papers there was not one which dealt specifically with song. "It may of course be said that song is not a detachable, independent subject and is bound up with music, dance and other activities. But there were scores of papers which dealth with much narrower subjects; there was one, for example, on Aspects of Dentition.

Or take another test. I possess about a hundred and fifty books on ethnology. Only four or five of them mention singing, and there is not one which treats of it at all adequately!"

That was in 1940. Forty years and more later the situation is not very much better. Tribal oral traditions have been, no doubt, studied and more of the poetry of the primitives published but social anthropology is still not very kind to the study of primitive songs as a method of sociological enquiry. Besides, these songs are not merely of interest as sociological literature; they have a lot of value as poetry. As regards Indian tribal poetry, Verrier Elwin's *Folk Songs of Chhatisgarh*, *Folk Songs of Maikal Hills*, *Songs of the Forest* (the latter two with Shamrao Hivale) and

W.G. Archer's *The Blue Grove, the Dove and the Leopard* and *The Hill of Flutes* have made significant contributions towards an understanding and appreciation of these folk songs and poems. In *The Baiga*, an ethnic monograph, Elwin made extensive use of songs as sociological 'documents'. As a matter of fact, poetry and ethnography are inseparable in this wonderful work. Archer's translations of Oraon songs in the two anthologies referred to followed the technique of Arthur Waley's brilliant transcreations of Chinese poems. *The Blue Grove* contained some of the finest translations of Indian tribal potery I have seen to date. They were done with a great deal of delicacy and revealed a high sense of intimacy with the Oraon way of life and sensibility. Mention may also be made of Hem Barua and Gopinath Mohanty's contribution in this field. Barring, however, these and a few other works, the picture, unfortunately, remains as bleak today as in the forties.

There have been no systematic attempts to document the oral poetry of the different primitive tribes all over the country. Analysis of the songs, the myths, the tales, the legends and the riddles can follow, but the first task is a systematic collection of these data which run the risk of vanishing into oblivion through sheer disuse and neglect. In each tribal group, generally speaking, the younger generation which has got the benefit of modern education tends to look down upon participation in the songs and dances of the tribe. Eager to climb the socio-economic ladder, they forget the lore of the tribe and, with the passing of the generations, certain songs also die and nobody knows them. Even within a decade I have seen proof of such extinction in particular tribal villages. In 1978 nobody knew or remembered a song which was recited with gusto in 1970 as the main voices, which has been those of a few old men, were no longer there. It is, therefore, essential that we collect all the traditional songs, myths, stories, riddles, rituals and cosmologies as early as possible, systematise them and analyse them, not as oral literature but also in relation to value-systems, social structures, personality traits and symbolic milieu.

These oral poems are highly concrete in their treatment of theme and generally refer to some specific aspect of community life, its myth or symbolic structure. In a sense, the entire community life of the tribal is a very intense and uniform symbolic milieu. There is, therefore, no problem of communication, no difficulty of aesthetic distance that burdens so much of modern art and poetry. For us in modern society the symbolic milieu has been completely fragmented. The mythical universe is no longer part of a living tradition in most urbanised communities. When attempts are made to resuscitate the myth there is a genuine risk of its appearing as part of cultural anthropology rather than literature. This, I believe, is the difficulty in Eliot's poetry. The Waste Land goes back to *The Golden Bough* and *From Ritual to Romance*, but society no longer understands or, rather, is no longer immersed in, the living myths of the tribe. It is, therefore, at best, harking back to an academic tradition; at worst an attempt to bring in too much of cultural anthropology. The difficulty of a return to myth and to myth-oriented literature so extensively attempted by Eliot and Pound, and given such stout critical support by Professor Northrop Frye, is precisely this: the roots of social consciousness in the West are no longer in those fertile, dark and primitive unconscious. But to the Munda, the Oraon, the Kondh or the Parajas the myths are ever present realities. Their poetry, therefore, is very much concrete. Take this Munda song:

> Dreaming of you in bed
> I woke and took to the road.
> Stumbling the stone
> On the village-road I remembered
> I remembered my caste, my gotra
> And stood transfixed.

The obstacle to love here is not merely a mental block. The stone is not merely physical: it is mental itself. The stone marks the point where the remains of the ancestors lie buried, the symbol of kinship and *gotra*. So when the boy stumbles on the obstacle, it is also a mental block. The stone is the ancestor and thus the song expresses a very concrete despair. As if the stone says, 'No it cannot be' and this denial may be more insistent and forceful than oral objections of parents in a traditional society.

In all primitive songs words are only part of a complex grouping of communal activities, namely, religious or social activities and dances. The accompaniment of dance with regular patterns of body movements or mimetic gestures with supporting actions like clapping or stamping of feet influence the pattern of the words. To this extent the songs which are merely word-patterns lose something in standing alone without the music and the movement.

In a pluralistic society the autonomy of the cultural groups constituting it needs to be preserved and strengthened. This strengthening cannot however, be achieved, either by looking upon the primitive communities as museum specimens to be retained tucked away in valleys and hills and to be studied by the 'civilised' scholars from the cities, or by seeking to assimilate them into the melting pot of the larger community by encysting them. The healthy attitude should be to see them, as Rothenberg observes, as "a series of communally-structured and ecologically sound models from which to learn something about the reorganization of the society and the revitalization of life and thought."

In these societies there is poverty but there is no public squalor. A Santal house, for example, is the last word in neatness and order. The delicately carved bamboo-rods used by the Kondhs to keep their tabacco can be envy of any artist. Tragedies abound but there is no disgust for life, no turning back on it. There is no fashionable pessimism. At a time when it seems to require courage to say that man can be happy, the life-view of these primitive communities has a special meaning for us.

Life for the primitive tribes may be cruel and hard. Occasions of celebration, of festivals and joy, only briefly punctuate a life otherwise burdened with poverty, undernourishment and exploitation. But still, life is looked upon as an opportunity, and all activity as a thanks-giving for all the beauty and sacredness of nature, the hills and the valleys, the rustling streams and flitting butterflies. Many tribal songs have, no doubt, no purpose other than enjoyment; quite a number have an ostensible social or ritual purpose; but the largest number is concerned with the quest of beauty and holiness, of dreams and fantasies which transform the sordid ordinariness of daily existence into something rich and strange.

Of the large number of tribal groups inhabiting Orissa, Bengal and Bihar, at least seven have a fairly large body of oral literature, including poetry which needs to be properly documented and analysed. In particular this is true of the Mundas and the Oraons, the Kondhs and Parajas, the Santals, the Hos and the Koyas. Some of the songs are of a narrative type: others don't tell a story but refer to some significant mood, situation or emotion. Narrative poetry largely relates to the cosmology of the tribes, their historical origins and migration in historical times. More important than these narrative poems are the poems associated with the festivals running through the cycle of seasons and rituals like birth, naming ceremony, attainment of puberty, marriage and death. The festival songs and a large number of the ritual songs usually accompany dances. As such, the melodies of many of the songs can be transcribed in regular musical notation. Working on the melodic patterns of the tribal songs of eastern India, an eminent Hungarian musicologist, Dr. Rudolf Vig has found close similarity between them and gypsy music. He has put forward the interesting hypothesis that many tribal communities of India were possibly the original settlers of Eastern Europe around the Caspian sea and migrated to India many centuries ago.

These poems or songs can be considered from various points of view. Since they are meant to be sung they are often susceptible to expression in musical notation. The scores of a few songs have been attempted by musicologists to generate an interest in this area. Secondly, the song-poems can be analysed also from the point of view of literature, their excellence as poetry. Often it is a poetry of symbolism and extended metaphor with a freshness all its own. Thirdly, often they have a ritual, social or religious purpose, be it the celebration of a phase in the agricultural cycle, a life-crisis or a normal social function. Fourthly, dance numbers generally accompany them and they deserve to be studied also from that point of view.

Like all oral literature, these tribal songs also undergo a number of distortions over a period of time. Among the distortions which are common to oral poetry mention may be made of the incorporation of stray lines composed of words borrowed from the events and situations in the context of development efforts in the tribal areas and the changing tribal scene. In traditional Baha songs of the Santals, for example, they can improvise to the incorporation of a line like 'The Babus have come, they have come in a jeep', to rhyme with the line, 'spring has come', welcoming the first flowering of sal and mahul trees with the advent of spring. Secondly, the traditional songs also tend to lose the wealth of old associations of peculiar, archaic words and are modernised by the new composers. This has happened to Oraon songs and also, more significantly, to Kondh songs. In the early forties, the well-known Oriya novelist, Gopinath Mohanty, collected the songs of the Kondhs of Koraput. He translated a number of them into Oriya. In respect of others he provided only gists. Forty years later, it has not been possible to get at the meaning of all the words of the original songs even in the villages from which these songs were collected. Being an oral tradition, its strength lies in authentic oral transmission from generation to generation, and as such disappearance of certain words, subtle nuances and lines from traditional songs is not to be wondered at.

The most fascinating aspect of tribal poems is their symbolism. Owen Barfield in his *Poetic Diction* puts forward the interesting thesis that poetic diction is nothing but the primitive, undifferentiated state of language, when objects are identical with, and non-distinct from the bundle of associations they give rise to. This is the key to the understanding of the nature of symbolism in tribal poetry and its basic difference from symbolism in modern poetry. Basically, symbolism in modern poetry is an attempt to look for the unfamiliar, the concrete and the strange in a world excessively devitalised by the drabness of familiarity and generalised abstraction. It tries to break the strangle-hold of the referential, representational and discursive use of language in everyday use. The world we live in is not the symbolic world of the primitive. It is mapped out, connected, intelligible. A sense of wonder and awe is discounted. For the primitive, on the other hand, social communication is itself part of the vast symbolic milieu in which he swims as a fish. The strange and the unknown peer out of everything and language is a method of gaining some control and direction in such a world. In a sense the entire linguistic structure is a symbol. This can be illustrated by any number of tribal poems from this region. For example this Munda song:

The mahul tree
Full of branches and leaves
How it made the paddy field look lovely!
They are cutting away the mahul tree.
You five brothers, save it, save it!

Here the subject is not at all the mahul tree. It is the girl who has been given away in marriage. The village will look desolate when she is gone. And 'they' are the members of the bridegroom's party. All this is never stated but always understood. Further, the brothers are not really expected to drive away the bridegroom's party. It is only a mock protest and a reference to the brother's role as the sister's defender in that society.

In an Oraon poem oranges are very cleverly used as sex symbols for a girl's breasts and the ripe, raw and half-ripe are described as being 'too sweet', 'too sour', and 'sweet sour' respectively. This can be compared to the Maikal Hill folk song:

He saw ripe lemons on her tree
How could he control his hunger?

In another Oraon poem:

To a tree full of fruits
Come birds to peck
Crows, pigeons, doves
And they chirp and frolic

The tree is the house of a man who has a number of marriageable daughters. The girls can also be sweet-smelling mallika flowers. The girls of village Diuri and Surmali are, in a Munda dance number, compared to ludam and champak flowers:

How nicely they bend down
The ludams of Diuri
How sweetly they wave in the breeze
The champaks of Surmali.
When moving in a line or running in a curve
What a necklace do they weave.

This kind of hidden symbolism in what is called the 'clue'

poems, is quite common in Mundari and Oraon folk songs but not in Kondh or Paraja songs.

The following Munda poem makes an interesting use of sexual symbolism:

Red alta on your feet
Yellow turmeric on the palms
Which alta field did you enter
Whose turmeric field did you go to?
Tell me truly, dear,
Did you enter a house of turmeric?

In Munda and Oraon society red is often a symbol for life, energy and sex. The 'sindur' or vermilion mark on the forehead and in the parting of the hair is a symbol of married life. Red also stands for blood. Similarly, turmeric has associations with marriage and loss of virginity. Entering an alta field or a house of turmeric, therefore, suggests loss of virginity or sexual intercourse.

In the Munda poem the 'well' is a symbol for the girl's sex:

There is a well at the end of the village
Its brick walls shine and glitter
. . . ... ... ... ...
The bucket went down and down
The poor girl how she wept
And wept.

The well in tribal society is very much of social institution. It is the club for the village women where they come to fetch water and exchange the gossip of the day. The well is a trysting place for lovers. But it also is often used as a symbol of the female sex as in the earlier example. A Gond song upbraids a girl:

O little well, you give no water,
Your youth is past
Think well, your youth is ended

While a Dhanwar song says of a girl who has come of age:

She still
Looks like a parrot
But the well
Is full of water now.

In most Kondh songs every line of the song ends in a refrain. This gives it the facility for recitation. Often a few singers will recite the original lines and the refrain lines will be picked up by the rest. In the translation, however, these repetitive lines do not add much to the meaning.

The Kondhs are fond of jokes and laughter. They appreciate other's jokes and can look at themselves jokingly, satirically. In the well-known Baile songs the boys and girls mockingly refer to each other's physical charms and personal qualities. While the tone is mocking and the song is only play-acting, there may be an undercurrent of the hard facts of life, either in old age or in some unfortunate marriages. The Kondh is thus capable of terrible non-seriousness and irreverence. How else does he face the trials of life which are only too many: death, disease, privations, tigers, wild animals and the exploitations of wilder men?

The love songs are particularly delicate and reveal the endless feelings of intimacy between the boys and the girls. The symbols used are often highly original and the underlying pathos deeply-moving, as can be seen from the following extracts:

1. Why then did you leave?
The dance in the grove is yet to end,
The cocks yet to crow;
Dancing to the tune
How gracefully you were floating along.
Sweet as a song;
And the jingling of your bangles
Had the soft melody of hailstones
Falling in the dark.
But in a moment,
What illusive mist or dark clouds,
What lunacy swallowed you;
You quietly left.

Did not you proclaim unending love?

Our intimacy that is
Anklet to the feet, ring to the ear,
Why, why then did you leave?

2. Life is fleeting
Old age exhausts everything;
As crops do not thrive well
On lands once cultivated
And again dug up,
In an old man's life
Joy withers.
So as life lasts
And hearts beat,
Come, let us enjoy
Let us play.

3. The old hearts still beat,
And we are alive,
Here in this ancient village
Of dead ancestors;
And so today we could partake
Of this great jubilation
This over-flowing joy.

Shortlived is the dance of an old man
Meagre the meat of the barking deer;
So as life lasts
We make merry.

4. Man's tragedy is alike
From childhood.
Useless iron is thrown into corners
The poor man enters the forest
Crowbar on the shoulders
Basket on the head
And life, only a tragic song.

The beloved is compared to the 'distant fire-play', the 'jungle fowl', the 'surging siali creeper', the 'esi bird of the forest'. She looks at him from the lonely verandah with 'a crab's silent stare'. 'She is a child lost in the dream world'. Their friendship is compared to 'ring to the finger' and 'anklet to the feet' and when she goes away 'the brass string of my dung-dunga weeps' and rings out:

> How sweetly,
> It rings out the agony,
> The bare, naked voice of grief.
> And I cry,
> Helpless, forlorn,
> Like the little girl
> Whose widowed mother
> Walks away with a stranger
> To a new house.

The songs are mostly confessions of intense love by the dhangda to the dhangdi or vice versa. Most likely, he will play his flute or dung-dunga which will call out the assigned name of his beloved while spending the night in the dormitory. The assigned name of his beloved is essentially a camouflage so that he does not stand exposed before his friends or the other girls in the girls' dormitory. Everything is promised: love, happiness, wealth. Appeal is also made to the sympathy of the girl for he will be forlon like a little girl if his love is not returned. Passion is hinted at in the blue surge of the moon and there may be a forcible taking away which is often met initially with indignation, then resignation and finally acceptance. For does not a dhangdi prize courage, physical stamina and professed love?

She is invited to "come, entwine me/delicate pumpkin creeper." A village where there are no dhangdas and dhangdis (unmarried boys and unmarried girls) is a 'rotten village fit only for dogs and jackals'. And thus the endless, dialogues, the infinite numbers of questions and answers are kept on and on in the nights from the dormitory to the tune of the dung-dungas and the flutes. Love names are assigned: Nilas, Talas, Lembar, and Dumbar. The flow of life rushes on despite poverty, misery and death.

The invocatory songs of the Santals and the Meria song of the Kondhs are almost reminiscent of the Vedic rituals invoking prosperity and plenty for the community. For the tribals the supernatural world, the world of bongas, of spirits and dead ancestors, is as real as the natural and social world he lives in. There is a benign or evil god in the neighbouring hill, the flowing stream at the outskirts of the village, the sacred grove and even the domestic kitchen. These gods take an intimate interest in human affairs and their blessings have to be invoked by appropriate propitiatory devices. Here poetry and ritual go hand in hand and serve an intimate and important social objective.

It has been typical of Indian social organisation that it has always sought to create such a living and growing community, which is in essence a community of communities.

Among different models of integration of tribal culture and society with the larger society emphasis was so far placed only on the theory of a melting pot with constant give-and-take and cross-cultural coexistence. The time has come also to emphasize the search by the tribes for universal human values inherent in their own cultural matrix. The search for the great tradition, for abiding historical values transcending the demands of here and now, point to this. This is a positive sign for cultural growth and efflorescence vis-a-vis the arid confrontation or withdrawal of earlier years.

There are signs of an emerging force of counter-alienation in this new search for cultural roots by the tribal groups. Overemphasis on ethnicity leads to a drying-up of sources, an anomie grows in the heart. A genuine awareness and growing interest in tribal culture will sustain our commitments to universal values which emphasise community, instinct and imagination and may even help us look at the city as a conglomeration of neighbourhoods or as Buber's community of communities with varying cultural patterns, beliefs and value-orientations fitted into a mosaic.

One of the consequences of a greater awareness of the cultural traditions of the primitive tribes can be to induce us to step outside the prevailing climate of over-emphasis on cultural relativity that has encouraged cultural myopia and ethnocentrism. It can broaden our very conception of art. It is necessary to remember that the forms called art today were not perceived as such in earlier times or by other cultures. As we know, even in the Western tradition one era sometimes did not understand another.

For example, in the twelfth century no one really looked at Greek art. Similarly the seventeenth century almost totally disregarded medieval art.

The intensity of life despite poverty and the pathos and anguish accompany personal intimacy, are reminiscent of Dylan Thomas' lines:

> And I am dumb to tell the crooked rose
> My youth is bent by the same wintry fever.
>
> Short-lived is the dance of the old man,
> Meagre the flesh of the barking deer.

Despite tragedy and death, the Kondhs and Parajas, the Mundas and Oraons, and other tribal societies have produced a level of cultural excellence where a highly complex sensibility gives rise to a poetry which is yet simple and couched in the idiom of the folk. The old man in a marriage festival remembers his earlier days:

> The old hearts still beat,
> And we are alive,
> Here in this ancient village
> Of dead ancestors:
> And so today we could partake
> Of this great jubilation
> This over-flowing joy.

In the words of Frederic Prokosch: "Men, patterns of moving dust, loving those familiar limbs, learned to think, lovely curves so tenderly shaped to receive and give closed their long eyes, their thighs cooled in the old tribal water and cooled their dreams in unending memory of endless years."

# 8 | Invoking the Blessings of Earth Mother: Rites of Propitiation in Tribal Societies

> Singing is older than speech. In singing the human being has always expressed his relatedness with his forces, with the totality of life. In his speech he expresses his relationship to things. Song is the primeval communion of all, the ancient amicable-inimical closeness of nature whose pulse educated its rhythms. Speech is acquired separation. . . Song is magic.
>
> —MARTIN BUBER, Introduction to *Kalevala*

## I

IT WAS THE golden sunshine of the last days of *Pausa*. Eighty-year old Sarabu Saonta leaned against the *sal* tree at his door-step and looked at the distance. The air was fragrant with the aroma of unknown forest flowers and *mahua* wine. Butterflies with multi-coloured wings floated as lamps in the golden sun. In the distance, at the end of the village street, the worship of Dhartani had started. Almost the entire village had gathered there. The houses and the village street looked empty. The rhythmic beat of the drum revived memory of his earlier days and Sarabu started reminiscing. He remembered his youth, his songs, the mad abandon of moonlit nights.

Beyond the village were the blue-green ranges of hills arranged like coloured palanquins. Ranges after ranges of hills and valleys; that was his beloved Kondhistan. Down below, the gurgling hillstreams with their crystal-clear water; the yellow *alsi* flower everywhere and the buzzing bees. He knew his physical body would grow old and be discarded. His soul would go out and return in some other form to this beautiful land of hills, flowers and streams. Death was only another stage in the eternal process of ever-returning life. The villagers, the known people, the green hills—everything would still be waiting for him. The streams would still be flowing and the sap of life would be still surging ahead when he returned. He was sure to come back again to this beautiful landscape, the dozing valleys and the gurgling streams. He could not remain apart from this glory of human life.

Sarabu brought out his flute from the house and in the golden sunshine of last *Pausa*, his flute called out the names of Nilas, Talas, Lembar and Dumbar, the girl-friends of his youth. Sarabu danced as if he was possessed like the Kalsi or the Bejuni; as if the Nachini Goddess had entered him and he was worshipping the life-force with the last drop of his energy. Sarabu played the flute and danced. In the honey-coloured afternoon sun, the village dozed; dark shadows danced before his eyes and Sarabu dozed off finally on the most important festival day of the Kondhs.

Above: Dharmu, the God of Justice:

Below : Dhartani, the ancient Earth Goddess.

This is the opening chapter in Gopinath Mohanty's classic *Amrutar Santan* (Sons of Nectar) the celebrated novel on the Kondhs of Southern Orissa. It begins with the death of Sarabu, the village headman. Sarabu may be a character in fiction but he typifies almost everything that the Kondh culture represents, a deep attachment to and intimate love of this world, the ancestral village, and life here and now and not in some imagined other world, of a life after death.

## II

Sarabu typifies the world-view of all those people who have been variously designated by scholars and anthropologists as the 'primitives', the 'indigenous people', the 'preliterate' or, as in our constitution, the 'scheduled tribes'. The world over they are those who have been slowly marginalised by economic growth and development. They have, over long periods of documented and unknown history moved, or have been pushed away, from the plains and the fertile lands on the river basins to hills and jungles; elsewhere even to reservations and earmarked habitaions. They are the poor, the disadvantaged, the educationally backward. But they are also the ones who are still in harmony with nature and with Earth Mother and its sun-laden promise. They still look upon life as a gift to be grateful for and to be celebrated; and this ancient Earth as one to be praised, worshipped and also celebrated. They are the ones to whom the earth is not something to be *used*, not a *possession* or an object for exploitation but a living entity, an object of reverence, and the relationship is one of sacred trust and loving intimacy. For they believe as much in celebrating one's life in this world as in remembering, adoring and celebrating the world in one's life. The sacred soil of ancestors into which one is born is thus a part of one's fundamental psychic experience of life and is part of its spiritual dimension. The earth, the land, the village enter into and are secure in racial memory and it is only an ethical imperative to worship the Earth goddess, the Mother Earth.

The Kondh sings of "Dharmu above, Dhartani below".

The Santals speak of Maran Buru the great god and of Jaher Era, enshrined in the Jahera, the sacred grove of *sal* trees at the outskirts of a Santal village. But it is not only the vertical perception of god above and goddess below. The perception also spreads horizontally, far and wide, encompassing the land, its trees, its rivers, its hill-streams and its birds and each of these categories in the horizontal range also partake, both of the above and the below, of the distant sky and the intimate earth. In Kondh belief one does not *belong* to a place until one's grandfather's bones are below the soil. The Earth indeed is sacred and it needs to be worshipped. It could be by human sacrifice so that with our blood our mother is enriched (as in case of the Kondhs throughout history and right up to the third decade of this century, when it has been substituted by the sacrifice of a buffalo or any other animal). It could also be by propitiation rites on different occasions of the cycle of agricultural operations and the season of the flowering of trees in the forest (as in the case of the Santals and the Mundas). The invocation accompanying the Kondh Meriah sacrifice and the Santal Bakhens (Invocations) are some of the most eloquent tribute and prayer to Earth goddess in

India's primitive world. We have also Karama, the harvest songs and the Sarhul (flower festival) songs of the Mundas' that celebrate the gifts of mother earth in plentiful harvest and the new flowers in the trees. These song-poems (for they are poems meant essentially to be song) reveal the intimate sense of togetherness and harmony that exists between man and nature in the tribal societies.

### III

The Kondhs, and more particularly one of its sub-groups the Dongrias, are among the most primitive not only in Orissa but in the whole of India. They live primarily in the hills of Koraput and Phulbani districts. The Kondhs were famous in history for the Meriah sacrifice. There are different versions of the observance of this sacrifice in ancient times and in the documents of British officers in the 19th century. There is the "Personal Narrative of Thirteen years Service amongst the Wild Tribes of Kondhistan for the Suppression of Human Sacrifice" by Major-General John Campbell and two other Reports, one by General MacPherson and the other by Captain MacVicar. These 19th century Reports make out the Kondhs as a community given to drinking orgies and human sacrifice, 'little removed from utter barbarism'. Worship of the Earth Mother, however, is almost a universal phonomenon in the primitive cultures. It has been quite a task for anthropologists to classify and study the different forms of this worship, their origin, development and significance and how they differ from one culture to another. It is not proposed to go into any technical discussion of this subject on which the literature is vast. It needs, however, to be emphasised that the sociological roots of human sacrifice as a part of the worship of Earth Goddess was not understood by the 19th century British civilians and army officers. Some American Indians, for example, refused to till the soil because they felt they could not wound the body of their mother, the Earth. The Sioux Indian used to say: "Must I mutilate her flesh so as to get at her bones? Then I can never again enter into her body and be born again". This is one extreme of the mythology of the primitives relating to Earth Mother. Other American Indian myths speak of a remote age in which the "Earth Mother produced human beings in the same manner as she now produces bushes or reeds". The Kondh, like many other primitive communities, always feels a mysterious sense of union with the earth. There is also something parallel to the mystical experience of autochthony; the profound feeling of having come from the soil, of having been born of Earth; in the words of Mircea Eliade, "in the same way that the Earth, with her inexhaustible fecundity, gives birth to the rocks, rivers, trees and flowers".

The rites of the Earth mother are thus reiterations of the events which happened in *illo tempore* in mythical times. The rituals of the *terra mater* refers man back to his primeval association with the Earth and the symbolic assumption of the organic link of man with Mother Earth. Human sacrifice was thus prevalent in many agrarian primitive cultures. Frazer has discussed them in detail in his *Spirits of the Corn* and *The Golden Bough.* Mircea Eliade has also documented many of these forms in *Patterns in Comparative Religion.* Here is the account of Meriah sacrifice in Frazer's *Spirits of the Corn*:

"The Meriah was a voluntary victim, bought by the community: he was allowed to live for years, he could marry and have children. A few days before the sacrifice the Meriah was consecrated, that is, he was identified with the divinity to be sacrificed; the people danced around, and worshipped him. After this, they prayed to the Earth: 'O Goddess, we offer thee this sacrifice; give us good harvests, good seasons and good health!' And they added turning to the victim; 'We have bought thee and have not seized thee by force: now we sacrifice thee, and may no sin be accounted to used'. The ceremony also included an orgy lasting several days. Finally the Meriah was drugged with opium, and, after they had strangled him, they cut him into pieces. Each of the villages received a fragment of his body which they buried in the fields. The remainder of the body was burnt, and the ashes strewn over the land."

The Meriah song is in three parts. It is the most important invocatory song of the Kondhs and always accompanies the sacrifice performed to propitiate the earth-goddess Dhartani or Dharitri. Its singing is a taboo on any other occasion. The British civilians mistook the significance of the sacrifice. They thought it was meant to make the colour of the turmeric the Kondhs cultivated more red. Actually, the sacrifice is a symbolic fertilisation of the earth; the flesh cut away from the Meriah (the object of sacrifice) being buried in the fields is only to this end. The Meriah is generally acquired well in advance and preserved and nurtured in the Saonta's (village headman's) house till the time of the sacrifice. It is given all possible care and attention. On the day of the sacrifice, the villagers go to the Saonta's (headman) house and sing the first of the three songs given below. They then symbolically purchase the Meriah. Symbolically too, in sacrificing the Meriah, the headman sacrifices one of his sons: for the Meriah has become his son. The second song is sung by the *Jani* (priest) as he inflicts the first stab on the Meriah. His recitation is usually followed by a chorus in which all the villagers join, and it is an invocation to Dhartani to bestow prosperity and plenty on the entire village community.

### The Meriah Song

In the first part of the song the villagers go to the house of the Saonta on the day of the sacrifice and symbolically purchase the object.

I

#### Purchase of the Meriah

O' our Saonta
Our village elder
Have you baby *kutras*
Have you got tiny fowls
Have you got sons?

The season has come
The season of Dhartani
The earth-goddess,
Give us young fowls
Baby *kutras*
We will buy.

This is repeated a number of times in chorus by the assembled villagers in front of the house. Then the Meriah is taken to the place of worship and tied to the Meriah pole often with the bird of Death perching on top of it.

II

## The First Stab by the Priest and the Overture

The following song is recited by the village priest and the first stab inflicted on the object with a pick-axe. The priest's recitation is generally followed by the chorus joined in by all the villagers.

Here we sacrifice the enemy,
Here we sacrifice the Meriah,
The goddess eats up this sacrifice,
The enemy is thus worshipped.

Let there be no loss for the village.
Let not tigers prowl;
The gods need so many bribes.
So many offerings.
Let no calamity visit us
Let all be happy
Let all live in peace.

III

## Invocation to Earth-Goddess (Dhartani or Jhakar)

Let no famine
Visit our land,
Let no calamity
Plague our people.
Our land and this earth—
Let them be in peace.
Let everytning be in plenty
Like the siali and gulchi creepers.
Let our crops flourish.
This offering we make
To Thee, O' Dhartani.

Let onions grow well.
Garlics grow well.

We commit no sin.
We have no guilt.
We only feed the gods.
We only feed the Mother.

To you this offering.
Let no creepers enmesh the head.
Nor thorns prick.
As we enter the forest.
This rope you have made
To tie the Meriah.
This sword and the axe you have made—
They eat the Meriah.

We have no sin,
We have done no wrong.
No crime have we committed.
Your blacksmith has fashioned
This axe.
You have given us the rope.

Below: Dhartani, the quiet Mother Earth;
Above: Dharmu, the god of justice;
And we offer
Only a small offering,
The land will be happy.

The Kondhs also sing the praise of their ancestral village and remember their ancestors on the occasion of a marriage ceremony:

The old hearts still beat
And we are alive
Here in this ancient village
of dead ancestors.
And so today we join
In this great jubilation
This over-flowing joy.

Short-lived is the dance of an old man,

Meagre is the meat of the barking deer;
So as life lasts
we make merry
we thank Earth mother
and our dear ancestors
whose sacred bones lie beneath our soil.

## IV

The Santals are among the major tribes of India. They are also among the most numerous along with the Gonds and the Bhils. They live in a contiguous area comprising of the Santal Pargana, Dhanbad, Hazaribag and Singhbhum districts of Bihar; Birbhum, Purulia, Bankura and Midnapur districts of West Bengal; and Mayurbhanj district of Orissa. It is a tribe deeply conscious of what it considers to be its Great Tradition. This sense of a Great Tradition seeks to recall a glorious past in which the tribe enjoyed material prosperity and cultural efflorescence.

The Santal is still very much in the lap of nature and natural phenomena inspire in him a sense of wonder, awe and reverence. The hill at the foot of which the village nestles is a presence. So is the forest and the *jhola* (hill-stream) rustling over its bed of stones and pebbles. The vulnerable village is protected by the boundary god from the evil eye and from the wrath of hostile gods and spirits. The village and the village-community sometimes unknowingly invite the wrath of these forces on themselves. Often the evil spirits or Bongas are spiteful and malicious. Their wrath may not even have been incurred by any act or omission; it may be inflicted on the community entirely without any provocation.

The Santals have a very elaborate system of invoking the blessings of the gods and spirits and particularly of the Jaher Era, the Mother Earth. Their invocation songs bear the distinctive mark of their culture. As a matter of fact, the Santal tribe's search for the Great Tradition is inextricably linked in their minds with the antiquity and the sanctity of their ritual invocations. There are sixteen Santal invocation songs which were collected and published together for the first time in Santali by their great spiritual leader or Guru Gomke, Pandit Raghunath

Murmu. This author has translated and edited with a Critical Introduction these sixteen invocation songs under the title *Bakhens*: *Ritual Invocation Songs of a Primitive Community*.

The invocations are sacred, and, like all sacred literature, there are certain restrictions regarding their singing and the persons who sing them. The village priest or the *naike* alone is authorised to chant the invocations relating to Erok Sim Bonga and Baha Bonga ceremonies. Of the sixteen, five invocation songs can be recited *only* by the priest. The other eleven can be recited by the head of a household. The system of village priesthood is hereditary in character. While the text of the songs is common and undergoes only minor spatial variation in the Santal country, each priest has a few prefatory words before beginning the recitation of the invocation. These vary from village to village. Each village priest has his own special prefatory line. This core or intimate line is the heart of the incantation. It is no doubt a technical line but it is zealously guarded as a secret and even the *naike* transmits it to his son only after ritual purification. When his eldest son comes of age, the priest transmits it to him, along with the text of the *Bakhens*, the singing of which is the prerogative of the village priest. Given below is the invocation to Mother Earth, Erok Sim Bonga at the time of sowing seeds; and the Baha Bonga, also an invocation to her at the time of Baha or flower festival:

### Erok Sim Bonga

Our obeisance to you, Mother Jaher Era.
On the occasion of the Erok festival we offer to you
young fowls, and freshly husked rice.
Accept it in pleasure.

We pray to you:
For every seed we sow let there be twelve
And let not disease attack them.

If they attack, please subdue them.
Do not allow weeds and grass to grow among our crops.
Do not allow diseases and misfortune to befall our village.

Bring us the rain bearing clouds in plenty.
Bring them in time.

Let the earth be green with our crops.
Let there be no hindrance to our movements.
Let there prevail among us
the spirit of mutual love and goodwill.

### Baha Bonga

Salutation to you, Mother Jaher Era.
On the occasion of the Baha festival we offer you
young fowls, new flowers, and freshly husked rice.
We beg of you to accept them with love and pleasure.
We pray to you:

We take these new flowers and fruits
Let there be no disease and sickness from them.
When we are out in the forest hunting
please make the animals appear before us.
When our animals, the goats, the cows, the cattle are grazing
let them not be devoured by wild animals,
let the tigers leave them alone
and let them return home safe.
Let not disease and pestilence enter our village.
Bring us the rain-bearing clouds in time and with plenty of
rains let the earth be fresh and green.
And by quickening the mind and the body
bless everything with new life.

The Santali girls, like all tribal girls, are desperately fond of flowers but they will not put it in their coiffure or use them as a garland until in the Baha festival there has been offering to the Jaher Era.

### V

The Mundas live primarily in the Chhotanagpur division in Southern Bihar and the adjoining Sundergarh district of Orissa. Like the Santals and Kondhs they too belong to the Proto-Australoid group and their language is part of the Austric family of languages. The Mundari songs, like the songs of all primitive tribes, is a part of the complex of communal activity which includes singing, dancing, ritual celebration and celebration of social occasions. The Mundas revere the Earth, "the goddess who gives birth to us and when we die takes us back into her lap". Being an agricultural people they worship and praise her at different points of the agricultural cycle from the sowing of seeds to the harvesting of crops. The harvesting songs go by the generic name of Karama songs. Given below are two samples of this group of songs:

(1)

Look, dear mother
        who is standing there;
Find out, father
        who stands, there.

See, it is the goddess of harvest standing;
Look it is the harvest-goddess standing.

It is cold outside,
        come goddess, come inside
Harvest-goddess, come inside.

(2)

The Karama moon is up
There is flutter in the house
For the festival;
They worship Karama
They have given up eating
Fish and meat.
They have planted
The Karama twig in the courtyard.
For you, dear Earth-Mother.

When spring comes to the Munda country, there is a virtual riot of colourful flowers. The trees fill up with delicate green leaves, the *kusum* tree becomes a canopy of copper-red leaves. The *Palas* and the *simul* burn as flames in the forests. The Munda, like the Santal, is very fond of flowers. The intense love for flower and the delicate feeling for them which indicate almost a personal sense of intimacy with the flowers can be seen from the following two songs:

(1)

*Chaitra* has come
*Sal* flowers blossoming on the boughs
In the new trees new branches
New leaves are crowding.

*Sal* flowers blossoming
*Sal* flowers blossoming
New leaves coming out
Densely crowding.

(2)

To the forest I had gone,
On the hill-top the *ludam* flower
Was singing and whistling.

I came back to the village
There the *kia* flower spoke with smiles.

The best things in life also come to an end. The Munda knows that after the Sarhul festival and the celebrations, there will perhaps be no food in the house; the songs will end, the dreams will become memories. Stark reality will stare in the face. One can see this mellowed pathos in this Song which comes at the end of the Sarhul, the festival of flowers.

You had descended on the *sal* flowers, O koel
You had come with the new leaves, O koel.

Koel, for rice and *handia* you had descended
Koel, for the leg of the chicken you had descended.

*Handia* and rice ended.
    You went away.
The leg of the chicken ended
    You flew away.

The Sarhul festival is partly a *vegetation* ceremony and also, partly a *fecundity* ceremony. The ceremonial bath, the stacking of rice in baskets and the offering of rice beer to the ancestors and using some of this rice for sowing is associated with fertility. It is also an invocation to Mother Earth for good crops like the Santal Baha Bonga or Kondh Meriah invocation.

VI

Czeslaw Milos calls it the unattainable earth. For in one sense have not we, through the centuries, slowly alienated ourselves from it and its warm affections? In a symbolic or poetic sense perhaps the Earth ever remains unattainable for we can never fully possess it, never make it totally a part of our inner Being. But the Kondhs, the Santals, the Mundas, as also the primitive societies the world over seem to think differently. They conceive of themselves as being an integral part of the Earth's body and soul and non-different from it and, therefore, the Earth itself is celebrated in living. And so they ever savour 'the fruits of this ineluctable Earth in what Milosz calls the garden of earthly delights' and for them, in Milosz's own words 'the whole round Earth resides in consciousness'.

# 9 The Suggestive Magic of Archetype: Its Relevance to Indian Poetry

CRITICAL OPINION in India has been generally ambivalent concerning the relevance of T.S. Eliot for modern Indian Poetry. The metaphysical content of his poetry, its emphasis on unified sensibility and objective correlative, its powerful symbolic structure, musical quality and the new dimension it gave to language are generally welcomed. But its essential peculiarities in style, language and theme are believed to be the products of an age, of the sense of ennui and the lack of a sense of value in post-war Europe as also its efforts to seek redemption in Christian values and tradition. Eliot and Pound are recognised to have initiated that most significant revolution in English poetry since Wordsworth and Coleridge, the two primary achievements of which are the acknowledgement of the legitimacy of 'organic form' and the rejection of 'public' themes determined by historical sense and particular social groups. But this revolution which avoided the two heresies of 'aestheticism' and 'rhetoric' is said to have served only a historical necessity. The excessive use of anthropological source-material taken from Miss Weston's *From Ritual to Romance* and Frazer's *The Golden Bough*, (particularly in *The Wasteland*), it is argued, gives to Eliot's poetry a heavy-weight look that is unacceptable to the chastened mood of the fifties and the sixties. In England itself there has been a retreat from the Eliotic style and theme, a retreat from its social, metaphysical and religious overtones to the more personal, more immediate and relevant subjects of everyday life. F.R. Leavis has largely withdrawn from the position taken by him in the thirties that Pound and Eliot were responsible for a major revaluation in poetry. Alvarez, in *The Shaping Spirit* went to the extent of asserting that Eliot's experimental techniques had no significance for future English poetry since they were essentially an American concern: attempts to forge a distinctively American language for poetry.

Alvarez in his Introduction to *The New Poetry* ('Beyond The Gentility Principle') drew attention to the series of negative feed-backs which, according to him, substantiated Thomas Hardy's remark to Robert Graves that "*Vers libre* could come to nothing in England. All we can do is to write on the old themes in old styles, but try to do a little better than those who went before us". The compulsions that produced these feed-backs and the consequential retreat from Eliot were: (a) the political realities of the thirties that ruled out experimental verse, metaphysical pre-occupations and brought about a return, in Auden and others, to traditional forms, (b) the anti-intellectual psychological probings into the subconscious and the unconscious, the consequential obscurities and the rhetoric associated with Dylan Thomas that refused to have anything to do with history and common sense, and (c) the Movement Poetry represented by Robert Conquest's *New Lines*, which according to Alvarez represented a *genre* of "academic-administrative verse, polite, knowledgeable, efficient, polished, and, in its quiet way, even intelligent". The editor Mr Conquest defined the nature of this poetry: "It is free from both mystical and logical compulsions and—like modern philosophy—is empirical in its attitude to all that comes . . ."

Times had thus changed. English society had transformed itself from the crisis-ridden, apocalypse-conscious, bored, nervous situation of the period immediately after the First World War. Threatened with the possibilities of a total nuclear war and annihilation of mankind it now appeared to poets that all that could be salvaged out of the ever-imminent terror were moments of happiness 'which once having been, could never be denied'. Mythologies and archetypes borrowed from Greece and Rome seemed utterly irrelevant. History did not matter. Myths did not matter. It was no use looking back into tradition; no use digging into its arid sands like pitiable ostrichs. Life had also become more placid, more comfortable, determined more by the ordinary facts of socio-economic realities and any talk of 'values' or *weltanschauung* and so on seemed not only embarassing but also a matter of hypocrisy if not bad faith. This attitude was partly that of a "postwar welfare-state Englishman: shabby and not concerned with his appearance . . . ; gauche but full of agnostic piety; under-fed, under-paid, overtaxed, hopeless, bored, wry" as in Philip Larkin's "Church-Going".

Hatless, I take off
My cycle-clips in awkward reverence.

Or, the pointlessness of the daily ritual of living as in Anthony Thwaite' "Night Thoughts":

Sometimes you tell me of your strange dreams.
Mine are banalities
Trudging down, trodden paths to find a heap
Of fragments unromanticised by sleep.

Reluctantly, I wake: shave, choose a tie.
These daily things are cheap,
The small wage paid to keep my nightmares small:
Trivial, dull: not terrible at all.

Or, as in Laurence Lerner's dig at tradition in "Tradition And The Individual Talent", an obvious dig at Eliot:

The past will let the present down
Unless we tart it up a bit:
Troy was as great as Manchester!
Hector and Brando are a pair,
And Helen had your raven hair!

Long live the past! The duty's mine
To see the blarney does not stop.

The use of myths and archetypes in the Poetry of Eliot was an endeavour for returning to the roots of human existence and finding some solace for the predicament of modern man through certain eternal verities. The myths and archetypes place human affairs of a period in the broader context of history so that the harshness of the present reality is understood as a part of human destiny. They symbolise the *fantasy* of the community and enable the individual consciousness to objectify its personal anguish and thereby to tolerate and even transcend the cruel fate. The emotional experiences of the community which crystallise around the myths and archetypes evoke a vision of the contingency of human destiny and help to communicate that experience which is both collective and individual.

## II

The retreat from Eliot and his myth-oriented techniques is not confined only to this country or England. In America, where mythological tradition and experience are less pervasive and real, as is true of all new nations, Eliot has been criticised for going into the realm of cultural anthropology to the neglect of the experience of common man in everyday life. The whispers of history and its mythological and traditional overtones are much less powerful in the United States than for example, in Greece, Italy and India. The memory of the community is not very long and deep and therefore, local associations of the immediate present are much more important than myths and archetypes. This perhaps is the fabric of local associations which was William Carlos Williams' reply to the Greek and Latin with the bare hands which was promised in the epigraph to Paterson; his answer to Pound and Eliot and others who in his view could not see the 'ground all blossoming about them' and instead went abroad to seek other modes of redemption. Indeed the wry echo of Eliot's "East Coker" at the very opening of 'Paterson',

For the beginning is assuredly

the end—since we know nothing pure
and simple, beyond
Our own 'complexities'—

suggests that the four books of Paterson may be "considered as deliberate counterpart of Eliot's Quartets: the eternal Pelagian's answer to the doctrine of original sin".[1]

At least, a general comparison with both Pound and Eliot is certainly demanded in these lines towards the end of Book I:

Moveless
He envies the men that ran
And could run off
Towards the peripheries
To other centres, direct
(For clarity if
They found it),
Loveliness and
Authority in the world
A sort of spring-time
Towards which their mind aspired
But which he saw
Within himself, ice-bound.

In his "Letter To An Australian Editor" Williams set up two kinds of poets. Firstly, those who 'think in terms of the direct descent of great minds', who feel a 'mind to mind fertilisation' arising from their massive reading in past writers; these men tend to compose in the forms of the past and even when they deviate from the fixed classic forms it is nevertheless precisely the established and accepted work of the masters from which they consciously deviate, by which they are asserting their greatest originality. There is another type, "another literary source continuing the greatness of the past which does not develop androgynetically from the past itself mind to mind, but from the present," a poet for whom both the fertility and the forms of his art "arise from the society about him of which he is (if he is to be fed) a part—the fecundating men and women about him who have given him birth".[2]

By 1951 the promised four books of Paterson stood complete, fulfilling the early dedication of "The Wanderer" and carrying out exactly the four-part invention announced in the 1st edition of the Book I: "This is the first part of a long poem in four parts—that a man in himself is a city, beginning, seeking, achieving and concluding his life in ways which the various aspects of a city man embody—if imaginatively conceived—any city, all the details of which may be made to voice his innermost convictions! Part one introduces the elemental character of the place. The second part will comprise the modern replicas. Three will seek a language to make them vocal and four the river below the falls will be reminiscent of episodes—all that any one man may achieve in a life time". Thus Paterson was to be a type of modern mythology, the myth of everyday life, the myth of the city which is the dominating form of social organisation in the West. There was no need to look for myth to the tradition. The living present was itself a myth.

## III

Thus the development of English poetry since Eliot has been characterised by an almost complete denial of the techniques of using myths and archetypes to delineate a contemporary situation. An analysis of the reasons for this may have significant lessons for Indian Poetry. Surely there is something strange when a style and thematic pattern used by a great writer finds no followers. Kathlene Raine has said that this is because in Eliot the mythological references and archetypal patterns were more of embellishments than organised experience integral to the theme. Reference to myths and archetypes in *The Wasteland* and elsewhere remained more of intellectual decorations than intuitively felt experience. But this does not go to the root of the matter. It is quite possible to think that the myths that Eliot used in his poetry were no longer alive in the hidden subterranean regions of the subconscious or the unconscious of English society of this time. In other words the real difficulty of the mythological framework in Eliot could be not that it looked to tradition but this tradition itself was no longer a living tradition. It might not thus be in the real, deeper experience of the community and might have to be dug out from the past and put as decoration pieces.

In studying the inter-relationship between social responses and cultural change anthropologists use the term 'cultural pattern' to designate pre-existing configuration of tendencies which determine the response of the members of a community to the new changes. Mr Golden-Weiser has discussed the value of the 'cultural patterns concept' in conceptual explorations. L.L. Bernard has referred to myths as the symbolic content which become effective in activating the corresponding pattern in the minds of the members of the group. Thus the symbolic content of myths and archetypes and their relevance in poetry or art have an intimate relationship with the emotional life of the community, its authentic primordial roots. As Maud Bodkin observes, "When a great poet uses the stories that have taken shape in the fantasy of the community, it is not his individual sensibility alone that he objectifies. Responding with unusual sensitiveness to the words and images which already express the emotional experience of the community, the poet arranges this so as to utilise fully their evocative power.[3] Myths and archetypes that no longer inhabit the dreams of the community may reduce poetry almost to the status of cultural anthropology. It can well be that the basic problem of Eliot's poetry was that the myths taken *From Ritual To Romance* or *The Golden Bough* were no longer part of the living tradition of England. In Indian society however, the myths and archetypes of the *Puranas*, particularly those of the *Mahabharata*, are very much part of the living tradition. The *Mahabharata* is still widely read in groups and one person reads as others participate in the emotional drama of the text. This is how *Ramayana* and *The Bhagavat* are also studied. One does not have to be a scholar or even a literate man to know the main stories of their texts. It is not my point that a knowledge of the stories is essential or adequate for proper appreciation of the poetry based upon the myths and the archetypes drawn from the *Puranas*, but it certainly aids their application and to an extent solves the problem of communication which has continued to be-devil modern poetry. Once the stories are known and their emotional atmosphere is understood the use of the same theme in a modern context may be easier to comprehend. Thus myths and archetypes drawn from the tradition may have great relevance for Indian poetry, from point of view of the problem of communication. Quite a number of stories and situations in the *Puranas* have contemporary relevance and an emotive significance of immediacy. In many rural homes *The Bhagavat* is still read as part of the daily ritual. *The Puranas* are thus not merely part of an academic tradition in India but are very much a part of the living tradition of the people.

IV

It is not as if I hold any brief either for Eliot or for the school of myth-criticism of Northrop Frye. I am quite aware of the limitations of Frye's 'Myth criticism' and its relevance to modern poetry, but, apart from the question of communication which has been discussed earlier, there are two other important reasons for which the use of myths and archetypes in Indian Poetry may be very much relevant. The first of this is a peculiar complexity of the Indian social milieu. It is commonly believed that the complexity characteristic of an industrial, urbanised society does not apply to Indian society, which is still primarily agricultural and pastoral, and does not experience the fragmentation of mind and estrangement characteristic of Western society. If in the West complexity arises out of the individual mind's response to the challenges of the external reality, in India the complexity is inherent in the tension between the metaphysical beliefs and social reality and also due to the juxtaposition of several social situations. The individual in India may not feel so much alienated or estranged as in the West. Surely there are not many Meursaults or Roquentins in India who feel themselves to be complete *outsiders* and who have no sense of belonging; but a society with thousands of years of history and often contradictionary, metaphysical and socio-religious traditions, can lead to a type of sophistication and complexity of mind which may be unknown to the West. Here is a purely hypothetical case. A middle-class Bengali gentleman suffering from tuberculosis comes to Lord Jagannath. He has faith that by continuous prayer and worship inside the temple he can achieve the divine grace. This feeling, however, does not remain isolated. His mind, faced with the delineation of sex and *amour* on the temple walls, is worried simultaneously about the crop-prospects, his domestic feuds, his inhibitions, the harshness of the priestly class, the need for funds that may be inadequate for the required period of stay prescribed by the priests. The quest for salvation remains immersed in the sordid and naked realities of social life. The pure white swan of Mallarme can swim only in the ice-bound pond and cannot fly off to distant Mansarovar. In India metaphysics and social reality thus remain together, interpenetrating all the levels of life and this can make for a real complexity and sophistication. The ambivalent attitude to life, love and death also adds to this complexity. It is not possible to go into the details of this attitude in this brief article. A brief mention of the approach to Death may perhaps bring out the essential difference between the Western and Indian approaches. The nearness of Death is an ever-present reality to the Indian mind. Death, old age and sickness are constantly present in our lives. It may be only a Buddha who renounces the world by seeing old age, disease and death, but it is the lot of innumerable lesser individuals to continue life's struggle after such personal confrontation. He is not insulated from disease, old age or death like the Western man. Old men do not live and die here in 'old-age homes' run by the State nor are they quietly carried away to the grave. Death and disease are harsh and naked realities in everyday life. Death breathes deep and the owls cry in the dark; the darkness almost whispers, death is everywhere squeaking and crying. It is not the fear alone. It is the kingdom of death that is seen. The village burning-ghat is mostly near the river and quite often on its sandy bed. There they are, all the rituals of living transferred from the warmth and intimacy of home to death's little acre, cold, indifferent, absurd: the mat and the mattress, the bed, the rags, the earthen pitchers. For is not the dead to perform a journey soon? And the river remains such a complex fate connecting life and death, almost a pipeline for the here and now to the eternal. Life-giving are the waters of the river, and life ends there also. The dead body must be given a river-water bath and sandalwood pasted on his forehead before the pyre is lit up. But the dead are only ancestors. They continue to live with us and have an unseen hand in moulding our affairs. And every year their spirits are invoked on the anniversary day and offerings of rice, dal and other foods are made. During the festival of Light they are invoked with burning torches: 'Thou ancestors, come in darkness, return in light.'

And so is the approach to Time. Indian life ever oscillates between the twin aspects of time: time as history, as broken fragments of moments, sequences and events; and Time as Eternity. The time of social reality is the time of objects, their misfortunes, subjectivity and fate; and Time as Eternity is that of which Krishna says in *The Gita*: "I am Time, come as the destroyer of the world". Tomorrow, said a Western thinker, is our permanent address. This is completely in tune with the Indian approach. This tomorrow is the ultimate vision of Hindu life. There Vishnu sleeps in his *Anantasayana* (the endless sleep) on the coiled heap of the body of the serpent of Time. Time is the sky, its eternal indifferent blue. Time is also the soft floating aimless clouds driven by wind. And those two 'times', the sky and the clouds remain juxtaposed, even in intimate relationship but ever detached from each other, ever unknowing. Western time is not so much riddled with contradictions. It is time as flux, the clock and the hour-glass. Thus the complexity and sophistication of Indian life that is almost inherent in the tension between Indian metaphysical ideas and social reality and is further complicated by the ambivalent attitudes towards life, time and death that add further complexity to this fantastic spectrum.

Thus complexity of meaning are natural in such a context and to describe these complex mental attitudes poetry can profitably utilise the unconscious forces, the 'primordial images' underlying the tradition and the social milieu. To quote Maud Bodkin again, "The approach through poetry, it seems to me, can bring new light to bear upon the great images that appear in religious experience: the divine man, the divine mother; Heaven and Hell; rebirth from death to life. Also, the realisation in varied forms, through the writings of different poets, of the universal characters of experience, in its inward texture and flow, may provide data/ supplementing or correcting the generalisations concerning the experience which psychologists working in other fields contribute toward the final synthesis of the philosopher". Myths and archetypes can thus provide not only the structure but also the substance of poetry that transmutes the universal experience of mankind through concrete metaphysical situations. They can operate both as a principle of artistic organisation and as the source-material which are universal because they are deeply and intimately personal. The time-dimension is transcended and time as history becomes non-different from Time as Eternity. Human affairs and events gather new meanings, assume new unsuspected perspectives against such universality.

Two of the commonest criticisms against myths and archetypes in poetry are: one, that in putting experience in a broader human perspective they take away their essential qualities of *concreteness*, *particularity*, *uniqueness* and *intensity* and what is left is an *abstract*, *generalised*, *universal*, *expansive* experience-pattern; and two, that they stifle the search for new language, new voice and a new tone by giving access to an established linguistic and tonal pattern. It is easy to see that these criticisms really don't go to the essence of poetry either as art-creation or even as a form of social activity. Poetry is not just experience in its raw undifferentiated state. The very fact of a verbal structure which embodies such experience can, in a sense, be viewed as an element of distortion. And the verbal structure can be endowed with qualities of immediacy, intimacy and power by relating experience to their primitive roots. The mythical structure is thus essentially a protest against positivistic philosophy, and a search for mystery of reality which underlies and interprets phenomena. The main instruments in this quest are the music of poetry and the poetic symbol as an universal central symbol or archetype in which, by intuitive correspondence, the emotional experience finds its truth and being. Suggestiveness and reverberation of meaning down the corridors of Time and the emotional life of individual men replace direct statement; analogy and insight replace logic. Myths can thus enable a serious artist to discover that much-needed middle path between the two extremes of over-formalisation almost to the point of obsession and a complete lack of stylisation that makes art an absurdity. Similarly uniqueness of voice or tone need not be stifled by adoption of an archetypal structure in poetry. Such adoption can on the other hand, give not merely depth but also originality incorporating a suggestive magic which reconciles the antithetical categories of the subjective and objective, the acute awareness of the isolated creating self with the world, unrelated and possibly uninterested and hostile. Thus far from leading to aridness, unreality and abstraction archetypes can make concreteness correspond with the secret springs of primordial images and help sort out the semantic explosion to which modern poetry has been driven in attempting to resolve the symbolist paradox that art is both concrete and obscure.

Modern Indian poetry, generally speaking, has been modelled on Western tensions between subject and object, between style and substance, between *intensive manifold* which is the philosophical justification of the theory of image and symbol as an aesthetic monad. Briefly speaking, it has reflected all the inherent contradictions and problems in Western literature and philosophy. There are reasons why the idioms of Western literature and philosophy and the styles and techniques adopted in Western literature have influenced Indian poetry and Indian literature. There is nothing to fight shy about it, but original creation looks for roots in the dark, deep and warm soil of what for lack of a proper word, may be put down as, 'local culture' and its world view. It is not the purpose of this article to argue that literature or poetry is a purely social function and different societies have got to have their own peculiar mode of poetry. But it is certainly its point that every community in its own strange ways seeks to express its deepest sensibility. Poetry as art-creation can be compared to an artesan well; when you reach the stored mass of water below the surface it comes up with tremendous force. It may be interesting here to note that two of the major poets of modern times, George Seferis and Salvator Quasimodo have successfully used the secret springs of national traditions based on myths and archetypes. Quasimodo, unlike Eliot, rarely used the long poem as his poetic structure, but his poems exude the warmth of Italy, Sicily, Tindari and its 'classical fire' to which the Noble prize award made a reference. The same is the case with Seferis for whom every stone of Greece breathes the life of Greece and every legend is a contemporary reality.

## V

In this section it is proposed to briefly indicate the themes and pattern used in *Ashtapadi*, an anthology of my own poems in Oriya. In reviewing it, *Poetry India* referred to its "sustained use of myths . . . subtly intertwined and orchestrated". To quote *Poetry India* again, "The effortless glide over historical time, the fusion of the individual sensibility with the collective, the kaleidoscopic shift of images and references, the blending of traditional, colloquial and modern styles, the emotional and imaginative range—all make this poem-sequence, by any standards, a remarkable creation". The reason for taking up *Ashtapadi* is simple: I can't think of any easier way of illustrating what is in my mind.

In Greece and Rome all history is contemporary and ever-present. It does not become a burden for modern man but a release, a source of identification with a higher realm of reality. Against the legendry and archetypal structure the men and women in the street don't become unreal; they only acquire layers of reality, varying degrees of significance and share different intensities of experience: The eight poems in *Ashtapadi* are really variations on a theme or rather progression of one single theme; the journey from the horror of hell, anguish and death, of painful, nightmarish estrangement of the protagonist from everything real—towards some affirmation of the possibility of life and bliss, towards some reconciliation with reality. In the first poem 'Dance of Death' it is the cruel, merciless fire of Time scorching the soul of the protagonist who lives only in moments and makes futile attempts at deliverance by traditional gifts, worships, and rituals. It is the terrible vision of reality that a pseudo-romantic, pseudo-metaphysical consciousness cannot stand. Beauty begins in terror. In the second poem 'The Child-World', the hell-fire is viewed through the eyes of a child as self-imposed estrangements, as the breaking of the toys of childhood and a curious inability to replace it either in dream or by, what Andre' Malraux would call, 'escape through action'. The third poem 'Man and His Earth' consisting of five movements, briefly hint at the possibility of deliverance by a kind of obsession with the harvest and indifference to history. It is based on the theme of Devaki and Vasudev, the parents of Krishna, imprisoned by the evil demon Kansa who was under a curse to die at the hands of their son. Their children are killed by Kansa before their eyes, one by one, but their obstinate refusal, in the face of death, to surrender, to lose hope, ultimately prevails. Death is defied and in that defiance the hope of conquering death dawns on the mind. The murder of their offsprings and their imprisonment is the symbol of man's history; in fact, as a record of failure, *it is history*. The fourth poem is "The Mid-heaven of Trisanku". Trisanku is a mythical character who hated the earth and its drabness and clay and being a just man wanted to be a god and to go to heaven. He got stuck up in the midheaven, neither in Time nor outside Time, perhaps in a blank space of eternal twilight, neither enjoying the deathlessness of the gods nor the sweet-poison that is man's estate on earth. In this poem the protagonist goes through a series of oscillations between the love of life and death-wish, between the aspiration toward saintliness and Don Juanism, and ends up in a curious moral ambivalence; a world without value where nothing ultimately matters. His own life is a pattern in this complete absence of value, a failure to find any meaning either in life or history. And then in fifth poem 'The Orchestra of the Desert-Road' the protagonist turns his back on life and the world of men in a curious feat of renunciation. But the desert is his own self; it is full of echoes and memories of dead grass; 'locusts at high noon' and dried-up ribs of time's caravan gaping at the merciless indifferent blue of the sky; the journey is that of the lonely soul through its unknown thirst. The sixth poem is 'Crossing the River of Blood'. It is the myth of Duryodhan; the ill-fated hero of the *Mahabharata*, who has to cross the river of blood created by his world-denying ambition and his flight to temporary safety for a day before his death using his son's dead body as the boat. Here the waiting after the bitter crossing of the dreadful river is only for physical death which at least can be a deliverance from the nightmare of hell. In the seventh poem 'A Song for Kubja' there is some ray of hope. The character is Kubja, a hunch-backed woman in *The Bhagavat* who is sick of her life-in-death, the ugliness and squalor that is her life, and in a moment of revelation, almost of divine grace, rediscovers the lost meaning of life when Krishna touches her. This however, is not a plea for grace or divine dispensation. The moment of truth is a moment of bitter realisation; it is the moment when intuitively the protagonist feels the bitter and terrible beauty and worth of life; the moment when it seems that there is after all something to live for. The last poem is 'Solon' in which the protagonist lives on an island off the seashore and has spent fortyfive years of his life almost as a part of the sea. The sea is life, a symbol of its violence, turbulence, depth and endless questionings. The sea is the medium of deliverance. Solon is all alone but is no longer lonely. In any case his loneliness is no longer an arid drabness, painful and disturbing. Below his loneliness is now the ever-recurrent music of the sea, the deep and complex turbulence of life that is for ever. The inter-relationship of life and death, the progression from pain and death-wish to an awareness of the terrible and beautiful reality of life and its solitary completeness and the complexity of this relationship is the theme of *Ashtapadi*. In the individual poems the protagonist is pictured as burnt-out in the fire of a modern hell. There is hardly any life or death here; it is all a living-death where the experience and distinction between sin and righteousness are obliterated.

The use of myth and archetype to describe a contemporary situation enables a deep and wide poetic experience to crystallise around a central image and helps the growth of poetic structure and form. In the growth and formation of life-experience space and time are perhaps not very relevant and from that point of view the life experience of a modern man is not very different from that of a man in the age of Mahabharata Homer's Ulysses is also the Ulysses of Dante or Kazantzakis only in a slightly different setting and context. And Mr. Bloom in the streets of Dublin is only another face of Ulysses. The Kubjas, the Duryodhanas, the Devakis and Vasudevas are not merely mythical characters. The situations in which they found themselves were not merely their individual fate. They live even today. You may discover a 'Kubja' walking the streets of an affluent city even while driving a Cadilac. You may see a Duryodhan floating or sinking on a self-made river of blood. They live even today in different shapes and forms, in different contexts and backgrounds. But the destiny is the same, the complex fate is one and unique, repeating in various patterns. And how often Krishna touches one's 'Kubja', hunch-backed, arid and meaningless existence when one feels that perhaps not everything is lost, perhaps there is still something to live for! The moment of truth is not necessarily the moment of God-realisation or divine grace. It may be the moment of the philosopher's comprehension of reality and truth; but it is also the common man's brief moment of happiness that comes like a burst of rain after an endless summer.

VI

Modern poetry is an exploration for the meaning of existence through the tangled impenetrable forest of everyday life. In Ionesco's words, "It is a search for an answer to the most unanswerable question about life and death; how to conquer the anxiety, to learn how to endure life and face death, sustained by memories of moments of vision". It is in this broad sense that modern poetry is metaphysical; not in any of the commonly understood sense of concerning itself with philosophy.

Lot of this poetry, however, has been the poetry of disillusionment and a search for values in a world without value. This is perhaps the inevitable bitter end of the romantic agony. Nihilism is the only natural result of the romantic ego. In the initial dichotomy in romanticism between natural and supernatural, between real and the divine, between subjective and objective, were perhaps the roots of nihilism, for nihilism is the nothingness of consciousness or subjectively is the foundation of everything. "The realm of modern poetry," says Mr. Miller in his *Poets of Reality*, "is one in which things, mind and words are sought to be rendered as *copresent realities*. The realm becomes more auditory, tactile or kinesthetic than visual. The disappearance or abandonment of the dimensions of depth and the separateness of objects from each other and from mind in an extended space in 20th century art provides special difficulties for someone trained in the habit of romanticism". The poem is no longer an idea about the thing but, as Wallace Stevens says, *the thing itself*. In such a world anywhere is everywhere. It is a walk barefoot into reality, an effacement of the ego.

Jung makes it clear that the archetype is something that emerges into mental form from the remotenesses that lie beyond the horizon of mental processes. He says, "The symbols of the self arise in the depth of the body and they express its materiality every bit as much as the structure of the perceiving consciousness. . . .The more archaic and deeper, that is the more physiological the symbol is, the more collective and universal, the more material it is. The more abstract, differentiated and specific it is, and the more its nature approximates to conscious uniqueness and individuality, the more it sloughs off its universal character". For attaining a universality without losing concreteness and the feel of immediacy, myths and archetypes have inestimable value. Carefully selected and feelingly used they can embody the gropings and inner decipherings, those 'impervious, verbal illuminations' which torture the existence of modern man and emerge as the idea of 'absurd' in modern literature. The private quest for value leads to some intimate, inward experience that can be communicated only in signs or parables and not *messages*. Commitment is universal and the poetry of subjectivity and the poetry of objectivity merely explore its inner and outer faces respectively. Poetry chooses fresh epithets and fresh metaphors not so much because they are new and we are tired of the old, but because the old cease to convey a physical thing and become *abstract counters*. If images and symbols in modern poetry are not to become such dead and abstract counters and mere decorations which they threaten to be as the inevitable bitter end of the Imagist movement, they have to touch and draw upon the living warmth of the myths and archetypes. That way they can convey the very essence of an intuitive language.

"The modern conception of art", said Baudelaire, "is to create a suggestive magic including at the same time object and subject, the world outside and the artist himself". The proper comprehension of the role of myths and archetypes and their effective use can give new dimension to Indian Poetry and help it to create such a *suggestive magic*.

## Notes

1. The Poem of the Mind, L.L. Martz, p. 143.
2. Briarcliff Quarterly, 3—1964, pp. 205-8.
3. Archetypal patterns in poetry, pp. 7-8.

# 10 Literary Criticism as *Sabhyata-Sameeksha*

COGITO ERGO SUM. I think, therefore I am. With that assertion of Descartes a new era in human philosophy and civilization had begun, an era in which the thinking, reasoning or rationalising individual because the centre-piece of reality. The objective reality had an existence and meaning only as endowed with by the human mind.

Maybe for the last one hundred years the wheel has been turning in the other direction. The explosion of knowledge and the unwillingness to accept the finality of any given truth as the ultimate, have combined to reveal the helplessness of the human mind confronted by mountains of information, facts, even knowledge. For Eliot may still mourn the wisdom we have lost in knowledge and the twenty centuries that have brought us nearer to darkness and death, uncertainty and anxiety. The primacy of the individual cognitive faculty is replaced by the dull and ever-invading eternity of objects, blind facts and the result is nausea, non-belonging, estrangement, a sense of vacuity and total rootlessness.

The windowless monad of the individual self-faced with uncertainty and anxiety arising out of the confrontation with what it considers a hostile and alien universe, tends to seek escape sometime in suicide or blind murder. Such a mind is the primordial *outsider*, who can be blinded into non-feeling on a mother's death or can kill an Arab on the sea-shore. Meursault and Roquentin become the protagonists of his tragic destiny.

This philosophical approach to reality has its reflection both in literature and the waning of the critical spirit in our times. True criticism, like true revolution, must be born out of love; out of an attachment for and a striving towards balance and order out of chaos and conflict. Otherwise, as in our sad times we have noticed, criticism may become another name for cynicism or nihilism and revolution, like the planet Saturn, eat its own children. The true rebel is the true lover; he rejects because he loves certain values or ideas very dearly. He revolts, he criticises because he wants to move towards a better perception of reality.

The waning of the critical spirit has thus a host of metaphysical, sociological and historical reasons which are already part of our times. The information and knowledge explosion; the media managers who are the economic gate-keepers to arts, the myriad persuaders of the world of advertisement, some hidden, others not so hidden; the inability or the incapacity of the human mind to comprehend and shift facts and try to arrive at truth—all these have inevitably conspired to both tempt the human mind towards acceptance of various creeds of totalisation which emerge out of an anguished feeling of helplessness and a desperate search for clarity, meaning, relevance and significance.

It is, however, true to say that creative literature like other forms of creativity and criticism, have also at the same time offered significant resistance to both our attitude of helplessness and the persuaders who, not content with ordering our economies or politics, also want to order our lives. This has been what Octavio Paz rightly referred to as the *secret fiesta*, a resistance of creativity to the brute forces of conformism.

But unfortunately so much of criticism in our times has tended to become either cynical, nihilistic or formal! The philosophy of formalism has found its parallel in meaningless emphasis on structure or linguistic analysis. It has bypassed eternal questions of greater realities, more fundamental issues of life and love, death or anguish; our times and its tragic dimensions. Critics have juggled with words, sharpened scalpels and knives but failed to either illuminate the works they are analysing and the world of reality they are viewing or build bridges of understanding between the works and the world and the reader. Repeatedly they have frightened the innocent and the credulous reader with their show of knowledge, turning the light on themselves or their theories rather than on the works of creativity of the world which is their context. No wonder they have intimidated rather than illumined; they have confused rather than clarified or led towards lucidity. They have 'botanised over mother's graves' and have forgotten the supreme need for a pair of eyes and a feeling heart in the mad rush for knives and microscopes. Reality has become even more distant. Shadow-boxing with pale images and paler ideas and theories have taken over. Historicism or myth-criticism is not the ultimate answer to human condition nor is language merely a gesture. Our condition is a function of language and Sartre was right in emphasising that language is our 'pincer', our antenae on reality. Language is part of the soul just as the latter is the stuff of time as eternity and time as history.

Criticism has thus largely failed to create sensitive readership in our times. It has failed to connect the *words* or the canvas or the melody with the *world* and the latter with our times and its ethos and reality. There are no doubt honourable exceptions but they are exceptions that prove the rule.

Rarely has criticism created a milieu for courage, innovativeness or imagination. Often it has sapped courage, undermined innovativeness and almost always been conservative. The pity is all the more that it has confused its conservatism as the only defence against nihilism and escapism, madness and suicide, lack of clarity and the field being made over to the creeds of totalisation bent on capturing and twisting the thinking individual. Where is the criticism that would insist on the individual's 'feeling', 'thinking' and 'positing' as the ultimate justification for its existence? Where is the criticism that would refuse to fall a prey either to helpless surrender, blind acceptance or brutal murderous revolt and rage? Where is the criticism that even while making us conscious of our tragic destiny would yet offer the only consolation available in reasoned analysis of reality and not like false prophets lull us into sleep, death, narcissus-like absorption or suicide.

Criticism has mattered to me as a writer but I have always taken it for whatever it is worth and have never been obsessed with it. The criticism of the average reader, the 'non-critic' has also mattered a lot for they judge essentially with the heart and the sensibility (and that should not be disparaged) and not with theories, book-learning or ready-made 'labels'.

Muktibodh's dream of criticism as *Sabhyata-Sameeksha* remains a dream. Today criticism is more often than not a parasite on creative writing and has failed to create a healthy or significant self-critical space within itself. No wonder the reader has gone after various brands and grades of false gods and economic gate-keepers of art who insist on forming the reader's or viewer's ideas on his behalf and are delighted that he cannot 'anyway' do much thinking. Yes, they seem to say, we must think for him. And their new motto could be in opposition to Descartes: "they exist because we think".

# 11 Translation and the Problem of Equivalence

TRANSLATION FROM Indian languages into English is a comparatively recent phenomenon and interest in this is partly due to a search for an all-India readership in different languages and partly due to the interest outside India in Indian literature. This latter interest, I believe, is, as yet, more on the level of sociology than literature; it looks at the translated pieces more as expression of the sophisticated and cultured Indian's reaction to the social milieu than for its intrinsic *value as literature.* The translations have also to conform, as fully as possible, to the usage and manner of modern English writing. Limited deviations and modifications in structure and use of language are often accepted as the inevitable price of this need to sound all right to the English-speaking ear. Maybe as more and more translations are done a distinct flavour of Indian English in translation will emerge without the need for hundred per cent conformity. A Tagore, a Kawabata, an Annada Shankar, a Gopinath Mohanty may have, after all, something strange, distinct and esoteric which may require change in the English usage and idiom to accommodate it.

It is one of the ironies of the Indian literary situation that a reader in Oriya or Bengali has greater chance of knowing more of Greek or German literature than say of Malayalam or Gujarati literature. The former are at least available to him in English. The need for an integrated approach at different levels, the universities, the Sahitya Akademis and other cultural associations to this problem is, therefore, great. The efforts in this direction are, however, extremely inadequate so far. The Akademis and the universities can do a lot more. We have hardly begun.

We may describe the translator's predicament in Beckett's words used in another context; to name the Unnamable. For each language this task of naming the Unnamable is difficult by itself because it is nothing short of 'weighing absence in a scale and enclosing emptiness in words'. This inadequacy is further aggravated due to a second series of defilements or distortions which are possible effects of translation. Words in any language can be looked upon both as *signs* and as *sounds*. As signs their referential context is the entire symbolic milieu of the community. Articulation through language is a symbolic action, a *gesture*. Words acquire pluri-significance, density and a peculiar set of associations and intensity as they live their lives. 'The force which moves the words and moves us' is the black force of gesture, of words as symbols. Every word is a cumulus of meaning which goes on attracting further meanings to it. Each individual, as Sartre would say, 'is *in a situation in language*, the words are the prolongations of his meaning, his antennae, his pincers, his eye-glasses'. The problem of translation is the problem of transferring the exact *gesture*. the precise *symbolic action* and the correct *sign* into another referential context. In trying to do this the translator may often discover that no such referential context is readily available or easily understood in the other language. This may be due to a lack of correspondence in apprehending reality and lack of equivalence in the emotional and imaginative patterns of the communities. In such cases there may be a temptation to convey only a general sense of the symbolic action or the gesture. This simplification is, however, a distortion of the reality, a defilement of the beauty and a mutilation of a perfect picture. Such distortion, defilement or mutilation may sometimes be inevitable, and the anguish of any sincere translator forced by equally inevitable compulsion to make available another vision of reality. What may be built up in this process is an *abstract counter* of meaning where words as signs or as gestures lose their real significance.

Then there is a second problem of rendering the *sound* of words. Different languages have different levels of auditory imagination. To establish a system of correspondence is extremely difficult. A crude example is the distortion caused to a song recorded at a particular speed by playing it in a completely different speed on a tape-recorder. The loss sustained may be the intricate music of words and the soft interplay of meanings and nuances to which this music refers.

I will try to illustrate some of these problems with specific examples from Oriya literature. Let us first take up the problem when the words have too much of referential context or gesture value. The origin of Oriya literature is generally traced to a set of esoteric, ritualistic poems known as *Bauddhagan O' Doha.* As a matter of fact this is supposed to be the common original source of Oriya, Assamese and Bengali literatures. Here a technical vocabulary refers to certain aspects of *tantra* ritual and the system of correspondence cannot easily be built up without explaining the significance of each word. The same is the problem in translating some of the poems of the famous blind poet Bhima Bhoi and a considerable volume of *Natha* literature, the love lyrics of Gopalakrishna, Banamali, Baladeva, Abhimanyu and others. Radha's separation from Krishna, the infinite waiting and longing for reunion and a series of other emotional patterns like *leela, rasa* etc., are very difficult to be rendered into English.

I am, however, not much worried by this set of problems because here the words have, in any case, more of an anthropological or sociological significance than intrinsic literary merit. The following translation of a Mundari folk-song by me will illustrate this point further;

> The Mahul tree
> Full of leaves and flowers
> How it made the paddy field look gay
> They are cutting away the Mahul tree.
> You five brothers, save it, save it!

The lines appear simple but they are only deceptively so. The subject is not at all the Mahul tree. It is the girl who has been given away in marriage. The village will look desolate when she is gone. And *they* are the members of the bridegroom's party. All this is never stated but always understood. Further, the brothers are not really to drive away the bridegroom's party. It is only a mock protest and a reference to the brother's role as the sister's defender in that society. Owen Barfield in his *Poetic Diction* makes the interesting point that poetic diction is nothing but the primitive, undifferentiated state of language when objects are identical with the bundle of associations they give rise to. To achieve this non-distinctness in translation is a supremely difficult task.

Another set of problems relates to translating writers like Upendra Bhanja where the primary emphasis is on the music of words achieved through a verbal structure too full of alliterations, assonance and repetition of the same words a number of times in a single line, each one conveying a different meaning. The charming musical pattern and alliteration tend to get almost completely lost in translation.

I had earlier referred to the temptation of using abstract counters and sacrificing the concreteness and intensity of the original when faced with the problem of lack of equivalence. This gives rise to a set of problems much more far-reaching than the two sets of problems to which I have already referred. Certain instances of the difficulty can be taken from Gopinath Mohanty's *Paraja*. The novel is an intimate study of the patterns of emotional relationship among a few members of the Paraja tribal community in the context of the exploitation by the money-lenders and petty officials. In the very beginning of the novel there is a charming description of the protagonist Sukrujani's house. It is not really a house in any ordinary meaning of the terms. The physical belongings inside are a few empty shells of gourds, a heap of mango seeds, strips of loin cloth and a few other things in that eternal semi-darkness of the extremely limited space with the over-hanging very, very low roof. In translating it, there is a genuine problem—that is, if the words are literally translated they may not carry any significance to a reader in English. What, for example, are mango seeds and why are they heaped in the protagonist's house? What is the hedge-plant *Baigaba*? What are the strips of loin cloth? But they are such intimate aspects of tribal life. Has one to explain why they are there, say a word or two about their use?

There are other types of problems. Take a sentence like this: 'When the Jaman shows red eyes even a pregnant cow would get out of his way'. This would be unintelligible to a Western reader unless (a) he is told that proverbially a pregnant cow is very aggressive, and (b) he has seen the way in which stray cattle can block a road in an Indian city. Or take the sentence 'The forest guard again came on his round'. In the original the word is 'Jaman' who may be a peon, or a constable or a forest guard but the association is of a very insignificant public servant on a petty salary actually strutting vain gloriously when he marches in the wilderness. And his coming to the village is not really a round or a beat. It has also nuances of a make-shift but elaborate camp-arrangement for which the tribal villagers have to provide eggs or chicken or other provisions according to a conventional scale of demand. We may take another instance. Every tribal of the Paraja group has three important names: one, his nick-name in childhood; a second, which the village priest (*Disari*) gives him on the basis of divination as to whose spirit (*Duma*) he is; and a third, which the unmarried young boys and girls jokingly assign to each other while spending their nights in the dormitory. In one sequence in *Paraja* an outsider in the village is told by a Paraja girl: 'So be it, I will be your Rice-flower and you my Red sand.' This will not be intelligible to a Western reader unless the context of village dormitory, the assignment of joking names etc. is explained. 'Rice-flower' and 'Red sand' by themselves would mean hardly anything. I had a similar problem in translating my poem 'The House'. In this poem the protagonist is confused as to where is his *home*, where does he belong? It is the room where his mother gave birth to him and where the ritual of the seventh day after birth was performed by embossing the clay-figure of the Goddess of Birth on the wall with cowries stuck to it? This is a concrete image in the original expressed only in a few words, but in translating it one had to explain a bit and perhaps in the process make it more abstract. Ultimately the lines ran like this:

> Even now in that corner room
> The empty shells burn on the wall
> Through the thin layers of mud and cowdung;
> And the Goddess of Birth looks at me quizzically
> From the niche in the corner.

The other difficulty in the same poem was in translating the protagonist's perception that like him, his son is also alone, seeking belongingness and that after putting out his funeral pyre his son is looking at the ritual lamp which burns for the spirit of the dead in the house where the protagonist was born. Here the lines ultimately were:

> Across the river sands
> Near the thin stream of water
> My son puts out my funeral pyre
> And scribbles on sand and cries:
> Who knows even now the feeble lamp
> May be burning in that corner room
> And the empty shells may be sparkling
> In the pale light?

I was not too happy but I could do no better and gave up at that.

The translation from other languages into Oriya has problems of its own. Here the volume of work already done is fairly large. There are translations from Russian, French, German, Italian, Japanese and other languages but mostly based on the English translation of the original. They are thus at two removes from the original and possible distortions are, therefore, greater. The translations are mostly literal. In fiction only the story is somehow conveyed and one hardly feels the impact of the original's style or the peculiar flavour of its language, its syntax or unusual usage. Such, for example, are the translations of Camus, Romain Rolland, Hermann Hesse, Grazia Deledda, Tolstoy, Gorky, Hemingway etc. The notable exceptions are Gopinath Mohanty's translation of Gorky's *My University*, and Anat Patnaik's translation of Gorky's *Mother*. There are translations from Eliot, Pound and Whitman by Gyanindra Verma. These do not, however, go beyond conveying only a general sense of the poems. No doubt translating *Leaves of Grass*, *The Wasteland* or Pound's *Cantos* is not an easy task. One has to remember the origin of *vers libre* in Whitman, the numerous references and allusion taken from *Ritual to Romance or Golden Bough* in *The Wasteland* and the obscurities inherent in Pound's *Cantos*. But here at least an attempt could have been made to use the considerable volume of critical literature available on the subject in the search for equivalent words and patterns of words, associations and moods. In addition, an attempt could also have been made to elucidate certain references in an introduction. For surely the translations are meant for Oriya readers who have no access to Helen Gardner, Hugh Kenner, Jessie Weston or Frazer. The translations do not reveal any attempt to seize the significance of the original; they read as mere paraphrases, as 'abstract counters' of an approximate literal meaning of the original. The quality of auditory and visual imagination, the rich intensity of the word-music are mostly lost. Part of it is perhaps inevitable but one is left with a feeling that a lot more could have been salvaged by more sincere and dedicated effort.

This brings me to my final point regarding the sincerity and devotion of the translator, his fidelity to the original along with his concern for the problem of the readers for whom the translations are meant. Thesaruses, dictionaries, and encyclopaedias can only be of partial help. But they are no substitute for patience, a devilish energy and a doggedness that does not give up easily, is not satisfied with easy compromises and glib solutions. The ideal situation is when three persons collaborate; the author, a translator who knows the original language very well and the language into which a piece is being translated also fairly well; and a final translator who is proficient in the language into which translation is being done. It is preferable if both these translators are not merely efficient in the *language* but also creative writers in their own field. This will help in proper appreciation of the peculiar thematic and stylistic problems of the original and help its imaginative reconstruction into another language without qualitative deviations.

# 12 Motifs in Orissan Temple Sculpture: Eros And Metaphysics

THE AMOROUS *mithunas* of Konarak, carved as they are in numerous poses with unabashed and naked realism have evoked considerable interest and criticism among the general public and the scholars, both at home and abroad. There have been all sorts of sophisticated attempts to explain (and even, sometimes, to explain away) these erotic motifs. Several clever hypotheses have been advanced to explain their preponderance on the body of the Konarak temple as also on other temples in Orissa. For example, it has been suggested that since, taken vertically, these lewd figures are found only up to a certain height beyond which they do not occur, could it be that the purpose behind them was to contrast the lower life of the flesh with the higher life of the spirit? Again, it has been suggested that the fact that these erotic motifs are found only on the exterior of the temples while the interior is absolutely austere and plain perhaps implies that they were meant to emphasise the contrast between the squalor, the fecundity and the humdrum nature of the world we live in and the peace, 'rarefiedness' and tranquillity of the inside of the temple. It need hardly be argued that these explanations are rather childish and certainly misrepresent the Hindu attitude to the world and sex as it was prevalent in those times. Another such clever theory is the Freud-inspired one of sexual sublimation of the sculptors of the temple who were working on it away from their homes and wives for years together—as if the sculptors were building or sculpting whatever or whichever way they liked without any royal sanction or supervision as to the motifs or subject-matters to be delineated on the body of the temple.

One point that has been discussed almost *ad nauseam* is whether these erotic sculptures can be regarded as a part of the 'religious art' of India. The inspiration behind this hypothesis and the supposed difficulty of interpretation faced by such critics perhaps lies in the fact that these erotic motifs are found mostly on the body of temples which are normally places of worship. It is, therefore, thought that they must have got some religious or spiritual significance. And the Western scholars and critics no less than their Indian counterparts have found it difficult to reconcile the austere, 'life-denying' ethics and world view of the Hindu religion and the vitalism and primitivistic orgies so often found in the sculptures on the temples which are places of worship.

The 'voluptuousness and passionate sensuality' with which the female figures and the amorous couples in Konarak were carved can certainly be traced, at least in some measure, to what Zimmer calls the 'Hindu ideal of feminine beauty'. According to him, 'the contrast of the extremely slender mid-portion of the woman's body with the richness and exuberance of the masses above and below—the great breasts and the fully rounded thighs—which latter, according to Indian poets should resemble in their roundness, firmness and resiliency the trunk of an elephant—has had for the Hindu mind a never-ending fascination.'[1]

The fascination need not be viewed as an expression of the *ennui* that is associated with most forms of cultural decadence. An affluent society always seeks to develop modes of artistic expression, more particularly in the visual and plastic arts, that cater to the needs of the minority of the *nouveaux riches* with leisure and the desire to enjoy life. Art tends to leave the folk idiom, the common touch and, like hothouse exotics, grows lush but lustreless in the windless apartments of sophistication and luxury Did Konarak and the other similar temples in Orissa, or for that matter Khajuraho, belong to such a period when the art ideals of society were dictated by the needs of the culturally decadent minority who, however, controlled the wheels of power? Or was it in conformity with the folk-myth of sexual realism that characterised the contemporary social values? Frankly, one does not know enough about the social structure and prevailing value systems and their relationship to contemporary plastic arts to speak with any degree of certainty. It is necessary to have more authentic knowledge about the contemporary cultural norms or religious modes of the elite which, as reflected in available texts of the period, both aesthetic and social, is still far from satisfactory. It is more necessary to know the life of the folk, their social values and approach to life, art and religion. Unfortunately, of this not much is known as yet. Zimmer takes a random sample from Greek traditions, the famous 'Daughter of Niobe' who has been hit by the invisible shaft of Apollo and the figure embodied the extreme tension of the lady and her juvenile charm rendered poignant by the hopelessness of the struggle and the confrontation with Death. What one witnesses in this classic Greek tragedy delineated in stone is the supreme anguish of the physical, of the flesh undergoing intense tension. The tangible and physical pain does not, however, reveal the darkness of the heaving soul, the 'mysterious operation of the life current and life-saps within'. Zimmer rightly concludes: 'Greek art was derived from experiences of the eye; Hindu, from those of the circulation of the blood; Greek sculpture developed to its acme of perfection through a portrayal of the handsome athletic bodies of the attractive boys and youths who won prizes for wrestling and racing at the national religious contests at Olympia and elsewhere. Hindu, on the other hand, in its great period, rested on those intimate experiences of the living organism and mysteries of the life-process that derive from the inward awareness gained through yogic experiences—and simultaneously had a definitely heterosexual flavour, distilled and refined to a subtle enchanting fragrance'. According to him the *mithunas* of Konarak certainly belong to such a period.

If Zimmer would like us to believe that these erotic sculptures have an esoteric religious significance and are embodiments of the highest conception of the dual agency of creation, namely *Purusha* and *Prakṛti*, Nirad C. Chaudhuri believes that the erotic sculptures in the temples of India proper, especially at Khajuraho and Konarak, have no religious significance whatsoever and are to be regarded merely as works of art meant for decoration and ornament. While admitting that the Hindus did mix up sex and religion, he is of the view that except in northern

Buddhism and Tantricism, this mixture is not reflected in Hindu art.

How then is one to explain the presence and preponderance of these erotic motifs on the body of the temples? Here is the somewhat candidly obtuse, but resourceful explanation that Chaudhuri offers:

> The Hindus did not look upon the gods they worshipped in temples as divinities in the Christian or even Greek and Roman sense. These gods were supernatural kings, created in the image of earthly kings. The whole liturgy of worship in temples even now is ministration to the daily needs and daily life of a king. He holds his lever, bathes, dresses, eats, sleeps, gives audience, hears petitions and praise, looks on dances, has amusements, and even goes out on excursions. The erotic sculptures are only ancillary to this routine and pageant, for if the royal palaces contained these, why should not a divine king have them?
>
> Moreover, the word *mandira*, which is the commonest word for a temple in Sanskrit and in the modern Indian languages, originally had no sacred association whatever; it simply meant a house, a room, or even anything that could figuratively be taken for a house or room. The exact sense was conveyed by adding a prefix to it. For instance, *deva-mandira* was a temple, *sayana-mandira* was a bedroom, *rati-mandira* could mean either a room for sexual pleasures or the vulva itself. The famous Sanskrit dictionary, *Amarakosha* includes the word in the 'city group' and makes the series of words *griha*, *niketana*, *sadana*, *bhavana*, *agara*, *mandira* synonymous. So, to think that erotic sculptures are a sacrilege in temples unless they can be given a religious explanation however forced, is to raise a fictitious scandal, of which the makers of the temples were blissfully unconscious.[2]

It appears both these extreme views give a lopsided and partial, and consequently inadequate picture of things. It may not be possible to offer any single or particular explanation for these erotic sculptures. The art of a people in general runs parallel to its world outlook and that way it is also a key to the psychology of a nation. In his monumental essay on the aesthetic of architecture and sculpture. Andre Malraux says: 'The barrier which stands between us and Egypt or Sumeria is no longer due to lack of practical knowledge, but to our ignorance of the spiritual background to which our knowledge should be applied.'[3]

The same may be said with equal justification about the West's lack of understanding of the background to these Indian sculptures. To start with, it may be mentioned here that the critical appreciation of Indian art began with European scholars. It is only a historical accident, therefore, that they used such terms as were already familiar to them. Indian art came to be termed 'religious' as distinguished from 'secular'.

And ever since, the critical appreciation of Indian art and more particularly the erotic sculptures on the temple-bodies have been like the proverbial seeing of an elephant by six blind men. It is not as if this blindness has been the monopoly of Western critics alone. It is sometimes not understood why at all there have to be clever explanations for some natural phenomena in the realm of art. Maybe the simplest answer in this case, as in many other areas of ancient Indian culture, would be the most rewarding and plausible.

In India nature is violent and elemental. The tropical sun is a torrid sea of heat burning away all life and the monsoon a veritable deluge. And the approach to life during the periods when these temples at Konarak or Puri or Khajuraho came up was largely pantheistic and vitalistic. It is in this sense that Indian art can be treated as fundamentally naturalistic. This kind of art, as contrasted with geometrical art, is based on a feeling of increased vitality, a process which German writers on aesthetics call empathy (*Einfuhlung*). In this art there is always a feeling of intense communication with, and pleasure in, the forms and movements to be found in nature. There is no withdrawal from the manifestations of life or nature out of awe or reverence. It is thus an art of involvement, rich and sensual, in the process of life, in the stream of blood and the sap of vitality. It is obvious that this art can only arise in a people whose relation to outside nature is such that it admits of this feeling of pleasure in its contemplation.

As contrasted to this, geometrical art shows no delight in nature, no striving after vitality. Its forms are stiff and lifeless, its lines cold and rigid. The dead sorm of a pyramid, the suppression of life in a Byzantine mosaic show that behind these arts there must have been an impulse, the direct opposite of that which finds expression in naturalism. Even an astute critic like T.E. Hulme goes wrong in concluding that Indian art, particularly Indian sculpture, was of geometrical pattern and shows what Worringer calls 'both a tendency towards abstraction and a mental space-shyness'.

'In the case of the orientals the feeling of separation from the world could not be dispelled by knowledge. Their sense of the unfathomable existence was greater than that of the Greeks. A satisfaction with appearances is limited to Europe. It is only there that the superhuman abstract idea of the divine has been expressed by banal representation. No knowledge could damp down the Indian's inborn fear of the world, since it stands, not as in the case of primitive man before knowledge, but above it. Their art consequently remained geometrical'.[4]

This wrong view is perhaps because of the fact that while Indian philosophy during the Vedic period and soon thereafter had looked upon the flux of events and the multiplicity of this world as unreal and was preoccupied with the search for the one single principle underlying these manifestations, at certain periods and particularly during the centuries when the temples of Konarak, Bhubaneswar, Puri or Khajuraho went up, the Hindu world view was based upon identifying life itself with multiplicity and the change and flux of nature. There is no fear of this flux or the multiplicity of images fleeting before the eye.

What did they mean to the
    men who are long since dust
Whose fingers traced
In this arid waste,
These rioting, twisting figures of love and lust?
Strange weird things that no man can say
Things humanity hides away—
Secretly done—
Catches light of the living day.
Smile in the sun.

Cruel things that many may not name
naked here, without fear or shame
Laugh in the carven stone.

—*Laurence Hope*

Indeed what did they mean? Who were those men whose strong but delicate fingers carved out these exquisite images in stone in Konarak and Rajarani and in numerous other temples spread all over the State of Orissa? What devilish energy and delicate care combined to give us such magnificent flowering of architecture and sculpture that one rarely comes across in the history of world art? To use Andre Malraux's phrase from his classic work on the subject, these voices of silence have spoken to art-lovers through the centuries about the hidden meaning that inspired the unknown sculptors and artists who took years to bring about such new dimensions of art-creation from mute stones.

A last brief point may be made in this connection. It is a fact that in India religion and sex life were often thought to have a close correspondence and books on religion or gods described their sex life in unashamed detail. The *Gita Govinda,* Krishna Leela, the stealing of the sarees of the Gopis as they were bathing in the Yamuna, the love of Shiva and Parvati—in these and many more instances sex is looked upon as the source and symbol of life and the love-making of gods is described in intimate and sometimes even lurid and violent details. In *Brahma Vaivarta Purana*, for example, Radha is described most voluptuously. 'She possesses solid breasts, great buttocks, a narrow waist. She is bending with the very weight of her buttocks, solid loins and elevated breasts'.[5]

The erotic sculptures are, perhaps, only the music in stone of such rhapsody in windy nights and the depiction of love as a storm of spears through which a naked runner has to run.

## NOTES

1. Heinrich Zimmer, 'The Art of Indian Asia: Its Mythologies and Transformations', pp. 75-76.

2. Nirad C. Chaudhuri, 'The Continent of Circe' (Jaico Publications), p. 261.
3. Andre Malraux, 'The Voices of Silence.'
4. T.E. Hulme, 'Speculations', pp. 88-89.
5. Brahma Vaivarta Purana, Ch. 124.

# 13 | Indianness of Indian Writing: The Sociology of Literary Imagination

ON THE FACE of it the topic may seem to be somewhat unusual. Yet often learned gatherings of creative writers, critics and scholars dabate and discuss it and go over the entire range of culture, social values and, what they consider, the *Indian tradition*. The conceptualisation of Indianness can itself be studied in depth as the sociology of literary values, literary imagination or simply as an ambivalence. Normally, no society consciously seeks to discover qualities in its literature which define its essence. It is a truism that literature, like any other expression of culture, partakes both of the universal, the timeless and the here-and-now. This, perhaps, is truer today than in any other period of human history for the simple reason that in the modern world cultural cross-currents have much faster mobility than ever before. It would not even be wrong to assert the emergence of some kind of a universal preoccupation with certain philosophical problems facing man at least since the turn of the century. Since Yeat's "things fall apart, the Centre cannot hold" to the Wasteland, then Sartre, Camus, Beckett, Robbe-Grillet and Borges similar or identical questions concerning human destiny, man's place in the scheme of things have continued to bother the more sensitive minds of this generation. This is perhaps true of all periods of crisis in human civilisation and, in some sense, there has rarely been a period of human history which its contemporaries did not consider to be the darkest. Ever since the Rennaissance with its emphasis on the Cartesian ego and Rationalism, the idea of Progress, Marxism, 19th century Humanism and the Existentialism of this century, one could notice some kind of a prevailing continuity of concern with human destiny in the cultural climate and certain obsessive preoccupation with fundamental questions of life and the predicament of man. This preoccupation no doubt found various expressions and styles in the arts but the compulsive fantasy remains the same, namely the apparent meaningless of life set in the midst of the indifference of the natural and the human world and man's ceaseless quest to discover, or at least impose, some semblance of meaning on it. What is important however, is the quality of thought and the idiom in which this metaphysical anguish and the search for meaning have been couched. This is the element of the *unique* which emerges from the cultural milieu and it is this in the literature of a particular language or of a particular period that gives its stamp of uniqueness to that expression even while dealing with themes or issue which are universal in their scope and content. Looking at literature from this point of view, one may start seeing the question whether Indian literature does not express itself in a typically or characteristically Indian way as a valid question. The question automatically gives rise to several complexities. Firstly, why should there be a debate on the Indianness of Indian literature when such a question never seems to bother, let us say the makers or readers of French literature, Scandinavian literature or Japanese literature. We rarely hear of speculations on the Japaneseness of Japanese literature or Greekness of Greek literature. The assumption has always been that even while dealing with universal problems there is something in a Tagore or a Kavafy or a Kawabata or a Camus which set these writers apart as Indian. Greek, Japanese or French writers. This is a valid point of view. Literature derives its excellence no doubt partly from its universal concern or relevance in its theme; it equally derives its strength and beauty from the peculiarity of style and the approach to life which is typical to a culture. As an example one may cite the peculiar quality of mysticism in the poems of 'Gitanjali', the vast Russian social and historical canvas of a "War and Peace" or "The Hero of Our Times". One could also distinguish between, let us say, the treatment of love theme in D.H. Lawrence and Yasunari Kawabata. Any sensitive reader must have noticed the qualitative difference in the treatment of love in 'Lady Chatterley's Lover' and the timeless and haunting quality of love as an emotion in "Snow Country" of Kawabata or the Sanskrit epics. Every culture has certain uniqueness of expression which is its hallmark; certain central symbolism in its approach to life and death; certain ways of looking at Time and its flux. Literature as symbolic action is after all, the expression of the inherent search for and relevance in a culture and this relevance cannot do without its specific form and style. The strength of an art-form is intimately linked to its ability to derive its latent energy from the dark and warm womb of its culture and to give it a universalistic preoccupation. In other words, one starts from the apparently provincial, the particular form and its anguish inherent in one's culture and seeks to give it a mould, a mode of expression that makes it unique and universal at one and the same time. All great art succeeds in achieving this.

Looked at from this point of view, the question raised by the topic becomes meaningful. Surely, it cannot be anybody's intention to give a cut and dry formulation of what is Indianness and how it has to be expressed in literature. For the complexity of Indian culture is almost a by-word. This is true of all cultures with a heritage going back to thousands of years. Nobody has perhaps felt this complexity more intimately or has described it more powerfully than Jawaharlal Nehru himself. In his "Discovery of India", he compares it to an ancient 'Palimpset' on which layers and layers of meanings, expressions, nuances and subtleties have been deposited by successive historical periods. The most important point in appreciating Indian culture is, therefore, to first become aware of its infinity, richness, variety and strength. Max-Müller in his own typical way had described it as infinitely absorbent like the ocean! Other observes of Indian culture have emphasised the same fundamental expansiveness of its culture. In which other country can one find centuries co-existing intimately at one point of time? Where else can one find a Rolls-Royce car on the wide streets of a metropolis coming to a halt because of idle cattle sleeping and meditating on the road? Where else can one find, in one the same family, the grand-daughter specialised in the most sophisticated branch of nuclear physics while the grandfather spends at least six hours a day in the family temple? Where else does one see an electronic scientist trained in the most sophisticated techniques beginning the day's work by putting a flower and vermilion mark on his equipment or offering a silent prayer at the assembly line. Possibly, few cultures have this kind of telescoping of time and history.

Another dimension of this complexity is the ambivalence deep-rooted in our philosophy, the dualistic approach to life and reality. Time is both history and eternity. All time is eternally present. Lord Vishnu is in His eternal sleep and the human approach to time and timelessness derives from this central concept of eternity. Faced with this problem of flux Indian culture devised its own concept of the relativity of time and a scale to measure it in *Brahmaloka*, *Devaloka* etc. The complexity of a culture can be judged from the way it looks at Time and Death. Indian culture has looked upon Death as only another beginning; a kind of primitive rite of passage. Mircea-Eliade has observed it so well that a long extract from his "Myths, Dreams and Mysteries" will explain it better than perhaps anything else.

"Let us now try to decipher the anxiety of the modern world, using Indian philosophy as the key. An Indian philosopher would say that historicism and existentialism introduce Europe to the dialectic of Maya. His reasoning would be very much like this: European thinking has just discovered that man is ineluctably conditioned, not only by his physiology and his heredity, but also by History and above all his personal history. This it is that keeps man for ever in a predicament: he is participating all the time in History, he is a fundamentally historical being. And, the Indian philosopher would add: this 'predicament' we have known for a very long time; it is the illusory existence in Maya. And we call it illusory precisely because it is conditioned by Time, by History. Furthermore, it is for this reason that India has never allowed Philosophic importance to History. India is preoccupied with Being; and History, created by becoming, is just one of the forms of Non-being. But this does not mean that Indian thought has neglected the analysis of historicity: her metaphysics and spiritual techniques have long since included a highly refined analysis of that which, in Western philosophy, is now called 'being in the world' or 'being in a situation'. Yoga, Buddhism and Vedanta have all demonstrated relativity, and therefore, the non-reality of every 'situation', of all condition".

(pp. 239-40). There is far less insulation against Death as a physical phenemenon in India than perhaps in most other countries of the world. A prince goes on tour of the city, encounters old age, disease and death and renounces the world. But that was ages ago. Every individual is destined to see death so often in his life, in his household, among his kins, in his village. It is a stark naked reality. Death happens in every home, in every individual cottage. It does not happen in public institutions in deodorised anti-septic aloofness and distance. The concrete fear, grandeur, pain and shame of death, the rituals accompanying it which make it, out as a rite of passage, stamp it with a quality of immediacy and sharpness which is perhaps unique except among the primitives of other cultures.

For the outsider, the tourist who comes for a very short visit to this country, temptation to identify India with what strikes him as the most important aspect of its life is almost irresistible. For him India, may be, the land of snake-charmers, *maharajas*, beggers, the *yogis*, the other-worldly philosophers, the erotic temple sculptures and so on and so forth. The list is almost endless. It is so easy to get a lop-sided vision of a complex and ancient culture. It is not to deny that all these aspects of the Indian landscape and the cultural and social life are true. But none of them by itself defines the strange and complex soul of India.

It will indeed be a pity if in our search for Indianness of Indian writing and, more fundamentally, of its cultural and social base, we fall into the same error as the outsider. It is also equally possible to develop an illusion of grandeur and to bury one's head uncritically into the past and glorify whatever existed. Leaders of learning and thought are not wanting in this country who are prepared to assert that any new thing under the sun—whether it is space-flight, electronics, para-psychology or existentialism—had their origin in ancient India. The hall-mark of Indian culture throughout the century has been its ability to critically examine the foundations of its own culture and to absorb, assimilate and make its own elements from other cultures and other civilizations which are apparently contradictory to each other and to its own ethos. This perhaps explains the continuity of the Indian cultural tradition while many other cultural systems have withered. But this has also its weakness: the lack of a galvanizing focus. One may perhaps define this characteristic of Indian culture expansive but without an intensity and focus.

Western world has generally looked upon Indian philosophy and culture as being other-worldly and not attaching any significance or value to this world or life. It is said somewhat glibly that the Indian looks upon life as a curse, a necessary evil, if not an illusion, and that ideally, human endeavour should consist in trying to emancipate oneself from its recurring cycles. This is only a part of the truth. Such a view would negate a philosopher like Carvak who held the material existence to be everything and observed that after the destruction of the body there was nothing and therefore, till one lived, one should live in pleasure. Indian culture is thus life-denying and life-affirming at one and the same time. This way one could notice the duality implicit in almost all aspects of the approach to life and reality: pleasure and pain, good and evil, life and death, virtue and vice, heaven and hell.

In short, the complexity of mental phenomenon inherent in the Indian cultural heritage is fascinating and its two major aspects are a strong sense of community and not only with all the living but even with the dead, the ancestors, and secondly a religious ethical over-tone inhering all aspects of daily life. The exposure to the external world and new ideas from the West have only laid a very thin crust on the traditional value-systems and beliefs of this ancient culture. The tensions that are generated in such an old and ancient society are of many levels: that between our ideals of socio-economic order and the many hurdles we have yet to cross; between the teachings of metaphysics and its general irrelevance to the social order (we are all brothers because God is our father but that is only in the other world; here we are divided into castes, classes, *gotras* and so on); between a glorious past of flourishing art and culture, a decadent barrenness during two hundred years of foreign rule and the present urge towards new artistic efflorescence; between a decaying faith in the indestructability of the individual soul and the myriad degenerations of the flesh; the ambivalence between the projected heaven of bliss and the prevailing anguish. In short between time as eternity and time as history; between social ethics or *sittlichkeit* and metaphysics; between the *Weltanschauung* a philosophical word view and the ritual of living. Modern culture and technology mix with the ritual universe of values and beliefs and inevitably generate ambivalences and complexities. This is the inherent strength of the culture and this is what keeps it going when several other ancient cultures have withered and vanished. It is perhaps also a weakness as it does not generate a focus of social intensity or gregariousness. But the uniqueness of the culture does demand a complex idiom, a correspondingly rich, complex and varied style of expression.

This is where I believe Indian literature is yet to go a long long way. There are difficulties and certain inherent limitations. The fact remains Indian literature is still a notion, an aspiration rather than a felt reality. There is no pan-Indian readership except for a very few writers primarily due to the problem of language. An educated average Indian reader in one regional language is likely to know more about Greek or Spanish literature than about the literature of his sister languages for the simple reason that Greek or Spanish literature is available to him in English translation. This deprives the Indian author from a sense of psychological being-togetherness with the speakers of other regional languages. This is no small problem and we have got to get over it. And frankly, even though the Sahitya Akademi and the National Book Trust have done quite a bit, lot more needs to be done to create a sense of a growing, evolving *Indian* literature.

But this problem notwithstanding, it is no exaggeration to say that Indian literature since independence has, by and large, failed to give a sharp focus to the complexity of the Indian cultural climate and mental ambivalence. Often there have been pale reflections or echoes of literary philosophical events happening elsewhere, mostly in the Western world. There was Marxism and the Progressive movement of the thirties spoke of class war, of bourgeois-proletariat conflict which, very valid as philosophical concepts in Marx was, however, utterly irrelevant to kinds of divisions in society, and mostly on the basis of caste, the divisions were not yet on the basis of class as a modern socio-economic concept. Similarly, there was Freud and there were many attempts to look beyond the gentility principle and the civic decor of everyday life to discover hidden libido, death or sex urges and so on. There was Joyce and 'stream of consciousness' had a field day. There were Eliot and Pound and lot of 'unification of sensibility' and 'spinoza and the smell of cooking' paraded as high poetry or literary criticism. And the latest craze would seem to be Existentialism of Sartre, Beckett and others. It is not my point that Marx, Freud, Eliot, Joyce, Sartre of Beckett do not or should not matter to us. Far from it. They are great names in the history of culture, literature and social philosophy. The thinking of this generation has inevitably been shaped and influenced by their ideas. Nor is it my point that they have no relevance to our social, philosophical or literary situations. They have intense relevance. But it is certainly my point that they should not find mere echoes or reflections here. They or rather their concern, should find a typically Indian expression. Perhaps one comes back to the question with which we began, namely what is this essential Indianness which can find an expression in art and literature. As discussed earlier it is perhaps the complexity and richness of the heritage, some essence of the Indian view of life and death, of Time and change, of pain and human destiny. And surely there are specific Indian answers to these eternal questions of mankind; typically Indian responses to the challenges to human intellect and emotion.

The entire question of the 'end' of life which cannot be separated from the quest of literature was also variously described. Indian culture, for example, never made distinction between the profane and the sacred, the religious and the secular. *Dharma*, *artha*, *kama* and *moksha*, each of this were equally desirable objectives of life, and salvation of the soul from bondage of life was possible through either *yoga*, namely the meditative withdrawal from the world and union with the supreme or equally well, through *bhoga*, namely the enjoyment of life and bliss of affection. Heinrich Zimmer has drawn attention to this duality in the concept of salvation and the dual methodology recommended to achieve it.

Indian culture has held an attraction for the West because of this complex and synthetic view of reality. Everything is a part of reality, every object, every event, every situation has its proper place in the universal scheme of things. This is very akin to the modern conception of reality which accepts its multi-dimensional character and our inability to comprehend even a small fraction of it at a given point of time. This is also in tune with the contemporary view of time in the sense that all time is supposed to be eternally present, and further, there are levels of time. Time is not the fragmented moments of Western philosophy.

A question may be raised as to whether literature has really anything very much to do with the philosophical basis of a particular culture or its social vision. True, no literature of a people directly flows out of its cultural climate or philosophical vision but it is the latter which shapes the approach to reality, the approach to life, death and time and therefore, structure the literary imagination and the literary vision. Superficially, literary imagination has nothing much to do with metaphysics that underline a culture. But deeper down the two act and react on each other. It is, therefore, necessary to take a careful and critical look at the Indian tradition and to realise its manifold complexities and its ability to change and adjust to changing times and situations. The risk, of the six blindmen seeing an elephant is an ever present risk, when one thinks of the Indian view of reality. On this latter question volumes could be written and volumes have been written. Suffice it to say here that the search for what defines the essence of the Indian view of life has to begin with a spirit of humality and an awareness of its infinite complexity which is both its strength and weakness.

Years back, in 1968-69 when this author was in Cambridge University doing a Course on Development Economics he had the privilege of reading his own poetry and speaking on Indian literature to students and teachers in London and Cambridge Universities and other poetry societies. Later he has had the opportunity of reading his own poetry and speaking on poetry in Germany, Denmark, Yugoslavia, Romania and the Soviet Union. A constant question that came up during discussion was the problem of 'communication' for the Indian author brought up on the best in Western culture and literature and faced by masses who have very little formal education. I had referred to relevance of myth and archetype not merely to give a focus to the complex cultural situation but also to overcome the problem of communication. In a discussion group Kathleen Raine agreed that whereas myth, sought to be revived by Eliot, could not go far in English literature because at the most it was calling back to an academic tradition, it was a very rich source-material for Indian literature as myths were still very much a part of the living tradition in India.

Indian literature may benefit by another close hard look at what constitutes the essential Indian view of life and a deeper awareness of the dark soil of heritage which is the true generator of authenticity, strength, uniqueness and vitality in all forms of art including the spoken word.

# 14 The Story of Ancient Dreams: More of the Third World

"The house is past. The only house available now is, though fragile and vulnerable, in writing".

—Theodore Adorno, *Reflections from a Mutilated Life*.

YES, THE Third World, of all of us destined to have been born on this little planet revolving in darkness round an ancient sun. It is our world, the same way as every little acre of this plane is ours; its past and its future; its tragic grandeur and muted voices; its shattered dreams and the new dreams yet awakening in the blood; its heritage and its hell; its struggles and its aspirations. It is our world, our destiny. It is our common fate. In every death we are reduced. Every birth we celebrate.

Our world here does not mean the owning up of the Third World by the advanced West. That world be a negative view symbolising patronisation and fulfilment of an obligation born out either of guilt for what happened in earlier centuries or a sense of charity and moral responsibility. Either way it would be prejudicial to the true and genuine human belongingness. As if the non-third world was now owning up this poor cousion. For, in a real sense, today no man is an island. And when the bell tolls, it tolls for each of us.

Whenever I try to visualise the Third World, I see a vast procession of shifting images that rapidly merge into each other. I see the Pyramids at Teotihuacan and on the Nile, the flourishing cities along the Indus, the Tigris, the Yangtse; I see Machu Pichhu, Tenochtitlan, the human sacrifice to the sun or the mother goddess, so that the sun rises ever young and the earth yields crops. I hear the chanting of the Vedas and the Upanishads merging with the wailing of the dying near the sacrificial altar. I see great civilizations slowly falling into slumber. I see human decay, the dark nights of the soul, the bizarre dreams, the sleep-walkings and the bloodsheds and the fragmentation of population, the new anthills of cities, fresh avenues of trade and commerce. I see colonisation, ancient civilizations now mere appendages to empires. I see the thumbs of weavers and craftmen cut off and a bitter night of darkness ruling vast landscapes in Asia, Africa and Latin America. I see a relentless struggle to be free, to break the shackles and to carve out new destinies. Political freedom comes but economic well-being still remains a distant dream. Once again they struggle, they flatter, they demand a greater share in this planet's riches and assets. I know of economists saying that the Third World is at best a myth, a creation of Western economic aid. They argue what has Brazil in common with Burma, or India in common with Nauru. True the whole of the Third World did not have great civilizations. But they shared an intimate folk tradition, a tremendous zest for living and an intimacy with nature. Today they also share a memory of long exploitation, an ancient and happy pastoral heritage and a struggle to ensure a better living standard for millions.

It has been said the world cannot survive half-rich, half-poor. The issue is indeed deeper. Should it survive that way at all? Must we dump shiploads of wheat into the sea as elsewhere people starve to death? Must we cut away more and more forests so that we can waste more paper? Must we keep on escalating the spendings on defence even as misery and deprivation stare us in the face? Must we wastefully continue to deplete the resources of this benevolent ancient earth as if we were the sole users and her conquerer? These questions loom large as we prepare to move into the next century.

The laws of history are sometimes cruel. The same history that saw the flourishing civilisations also puts them to slumber. The Aztecs, the Mayans, the Sumerians, the Egyptians, the Aryans . . . And when they awoke it was to a different order of reality. The golden age was always in the past. The gap between the dreams of the past and the stark reality of the present is so wide that often there is a terrible sense of illusion. The illusion of not belonging anywhere. Neither to the today nor to the yesterday. You tend to deny both. On rare occasions only you have the courage to merge them and weld them into a possible tomorrow of new dreams.

Despair and cynicism are pervasive and contagious. The creative artist, however, believes that hope and dream, love and compassion, are also contagious. And he owes it to his art to rekindle the little lamps of hope in the midst of growing darkness, to assert that not everything is lost and that tomorrows exist. To revive, resurrect and reawaken; to dream ancient dreams and derive sustenance from them – this is the urge within him. He owes it to his craft to balance the dream with reality and not paint an illusory rosy picture. He, however, knows dreams die hard and dreams are born out of today's darkness, its sighs and deprivations. From history he is not prepared to take on any bitterness, for of that there has been enough. His words are charged with love and compassion, hope and dream for all men, anywhere on this earth. His revolt is also born out of an intense love for the living.

And all this because he understands history. It is true his obsession is with the present harvest and not with dreams of the past but he also knows and values the presentness of the past. He knows where the roots are in the dark soils of culture. There could, therefore, be sometimes a process, as it were, of re-learning. A Max-Müller could make India look afresh and with a new relevance at the Vedas and the Upanishad. An Andre Malraux may listen again to the voices of silence and discover the beauty of a Khmer head and the remarkable monuments of Angkor Vat. The pyramids and the sphinx on the Nile, the monuments of Rameses and so much other heritage could be discovered by Western scholars, art-historians and archaeologists. And imagine China, which was the creator of a professional civil service based on merit—the Mandarins—perhaps returning to it via western models! The rise and fall of civilizations are matters of history. Toynbee has spoken of them. Pitirim Sorokin has documented the rhythms of its dynamics.

Today, even while the heritage beckons, poverty and low per capita income, unemployment and over-population, characterise most of the so-called Third World. In fact the World Development Report, 1987 brought out by World Bank speaks of a

Fourth World, including under that category thirtyseven 'least-developed countries' taken from out of the earlier list of the Third World countries. And as expected Ethiopia heads that list. With continuing famine and unending civil war this unfortunate country where Rimbaud had sought a new life after saying good-by to poetry—"that tomfoolery I gave up long ego"—is today the most telling symbol of poverty and mass starvation.

Some economists have spoken of the 'Matthew effect' in World poverty. They quote the Bible: "For whosoever hath, to him shall be given and he shall have more abundance; but who-ever hath not from him shalt be taken away even that he hath". (Matthew 13:12) To me, as a poet this is hardly something to feel happy. Even otherwise the Third World—a designation about which I have my own reservations—will one day surely find its destiny and carve out new pathways to development that may marry economic well-being to a happy and contented polity where the social web is strong and intimate. It will discover a mode to marry the city and the jungle; the enormity of speed with the still centre of life. For man needs a social system, a polity that avoids tensions and conflicts between groups and classes, between haves and havenots.

Each for all and all for each. It is only that way we can truly inherit the world and be worthy of its sunladen promise. To be here in this world is itself a grace and we cannot sin against life by turning our backs on it in despair. In the Third World today several centuries co-exist, several demands clash. Soon perhaps they will find their balance. We will join shoulders, give a smile, a helping hand as they restructure their destinities. That way not only the Third World but this whole planet will really become our world. We can embrace it in the awakening of new dreams that defy death and meanness and make possible love and compassion. And then this little world of ours, this tiny speck hurtling down through enormous dark space in the sky, will become our world of each one of us and belonging to all. Like the moon, the stars, like the sun that warms us all and the clouds that bring life-giving rain.

# 15 Tradition, Bondage and Freedom

THE RELATIONSHIP of Tradition to the freedom of the artist and writer, or freedom in society in general, is an ambivalent one. We may be living at a time when the compulsive burdens of the present, the here and the now may make one feel that really history does not matter, yesterdays do not matter, myths and archetypes about them do not matter, vacuous dreams of tomorrows also do not matter. Laurence Lerner's dig at tradition in "Tradition and the Individual Talent" is an obvious dig at Eliot:

> The past will let the present down
> Unless we tart it up a bit:
> Troy was as great as Manchester!
> Hector and Brando are a pair,
> And Helen had your raven hair!
> Long live the past! The duty's mine
> To see the blarney does not stop.

However Tradition does not always let down the present or subdue and restrict free expression or the free flowering of individual talent. Even if one does not agree with Eliot's emphasis on the intimate and causal nexus between tradition and individual talent, it is still possible to point out that the spirit of individual freedom is sometimes sustained and nurtured by pride in the heritage of a community, its traditional values and belief-systems which provide an antidote to current deprivations and degenerations. While to the unthinking, tradition can be a cage, a stultifying burden, to others, more particularly in times of crisis and heart-search, it can open up ancient corridors of excellence and faith and nurture the fight against decay and death. History is not always the enemy of the present harvest nor tradition the natural opponent of freedom or innovation. The problem can also be viewed from another angle. The human mind has always operated between a binary relationship between opposing emotions—to be one self, to be completely free; and to depend on others, to derive hope, consolidation and faith from such human dependence. Hell is sometimes defined as the 'self', and sometimes as 'the other'. When the self is liberated from different anchorages, roots (or call them bondages) it has to fend for itself in an environment which is hostile or indifferent. This is what explains all the talk about rootlessness, *angst*, non-belonging, alienation and estrangement. Such an alienated self may suffer from what Erich Fromm designated as 'fear of freedom'. Cut away from all roots, traditions, shared values and shared destinies one may float as a speck of dust in the wind. And such individuals are easy subjects for manipulation by the hidden persuaders, the media-managers, the economic gate-keepers of art, notoriously active in our time. Individual freedom can be a casualty in such a situation as it can be also in the other extreme of uncritical ever-dependence or blind adulation of history and tradition. The new forces of dehumanisation can easily kill the instinct for freedom and self-expression.

Freedom in society and the freedom of the artist have thus to be sought not in a denial of tradition nor uncritical ostrich-like hiding it. It cannot also be found in a systematic denial or destruction of all roots, corresponding to the 'complete derangement of the senses' of which Rimbaud spoke of regarding the individual psyche. It has to be found in our ability to acquire a capacity to experience reality creatively, intuitively and not allow ourselves to be deadened by the routine, the quotidian. The capacity to find freshness in experience, in the very ordinariness of life and its events is the essence of the creative process and that is why genuine creativity is always anti-slavery, anti-establishment; a 'secret fiesta' as Octavio Paz would say.

When Dylan Thomas said, "I am lots of people," he was, almost without meaning it, contradicting the hermetic tradition in art and literature and its pre-occupation with the private ego of the artist as the only valid approach to reality. The latter was based on an inadequate understanding of the Cartesian dictum *cogito ergo sum* and the role of the thinking process in the structure of human personality and culture.

The 'self' as the inner identity that takes a view on objects, otherselves, events and ideas has held away in Western philosophy and literature ever since Descartes. The intensity of individual perception and the approach to reality as the external phenomenon 'out there' gave us at least two centuries of rapid advancement in human knowledge, science and technology and the explosion of information.

But human intellect has gradually come to realise its limitations in trying to comprehend the ever-growing complexities of reality. Rationalism came to mean an indictment of intuition on the one hand and emphasis on the 'self' or the ego on the other. The intuitive and imaginative aspects of the human mind and its capacity to dream came to be despised. It had been assumed that truth can be seen only through the application of objective logic.

The reaction to this came from the philosophers of the irrational, the symbolists, the impressionist painters and poets like Rimbaud, who told us that truth is like a delicate flower that cannot stand the analysis of logic and cognitive semantics. It has to be felt in the heart and in the blood-stream, in the life of imagination and dream. The delicate nuances of truth cannot be caught in the wire-mesh of rationalism and cold logic. From this came the talk of derangement of the senses, the emphasis on intuition and passion, the dark forces of the subconscious and the unconscious.

Meanwhile, advancement of learning in the field of psychology and anthropology told us more about the structure of the human mind and personality, his submergence in the ritualistic milieu of social process and symbolic actions. The individual 'ego' came to be realised as a mixed agent; as much of direct perception as intended or unintended distortion. Social life came to be seen, to a significant extent, as a masked dance in which the perceiving 'ego' was as much 'masked' as the 'other' it perceived.

All this has become a part of the intellectual climate of our times but its link with the vision of man in art and literature is scarcely discussed. Traditionally, it was assumed that the artist had to be at some 'remove' from raw experience and the field of social action. His 'ego' was his room of creativity and through its window he perceived the sky, the clouds, objects and men in the street; in short, the life outside.

True, art cannot be an experience in the raw; the medium itself imposes restrictions. The concept of aesthetic distance is real. After all the artist cannot just join the crowd in the street and expect his slogans to be literature.

The point, however, is not whether the artist's position is in the room of his creative self or in the street of social action. That is an artificial and superficial dischotomy. Any true artist is, all the time, both in the room and in the street. It is not a question of either/or. It is not as if the writer, from his cool sequestered existence, from his 'safe' aesthetic distance from the turbulence of life, can any longer perceive it, collect his emotion in tranquillity and then give his vision of life and death to the masses of his readers. Nor can he show the way, pose as the elite and assume the messianic role, the role of one who is possessed of the spirit, the dark force of duende, as Lorca called it, or of the shaman or kalisi as our primitive people or the folk-society put it.

He knows that there are no walls any more. His 'ego' lives in a room without walls and roof, right in the street and right under the open sky. That is where actions take place, dust-storms rage, slogans are shouted, the intricate web of social relationships are lived out with all their colour, excellences and crudities. That is where dreams have to be dreamt. A folk saying ridicules the possibility of acquiring "the knowledge of *brahman* in the market place". That precisely is the complex situation of the writer today; *brahman* has to be meditated in the market place.

And yet would it not still be right to say that there is always a formal distance between experience and art? Even apart from the media imposing restrictions, the fact remains that the artist's response to the happenings around, to the life in society, in the street, has a qualitative uniqueness, if he is at all an artist worth the name. He has the capacity to perceive experience as integral, undifferentiated 'whole', and as immediately and concretely as a chill on the skin or an apple in the mouth. His capacity to transform the dust into gold still remains. He can still invest language with a magic which the language of utilitarian social communication scarcely possesses.

This is the quality of 'transluence' or 'opacity'. The purely transparent language of rhetoric, bereft of all dark shadows of associations, racial memories, insinuations, agonising suggestions, intricate symbolisms and allusions will be the language of slogans which communicate most rapidly. On the other hand, the language of art, even while it tries to approximate to the quality of common speech, seeks to retain this magical quality of 'opacity', of layers of meaning, of layers of nuances and associations.

This arises not from a simple awareness that one is in the street, immersed in the present, in the historical time and in concrete day-to-day events; this awareness after all, is common to all those who are in the street, living and experiencing in the raw, unable to put it either in the perspective of time or against the life of the imagination. The artist's awareness calls him back to his profession; to be still able to dream in the midst of the bustle, to find the relevance of action to the quality of the dream; to be still able to be a 'seer', a 'visionary' while being the man next door; to dream and yet to know that all dreams are basically illusions and must end.

As Kafka once put it so admirably: "a true creative writer does not whimper lyrics like freezing children, or wait ecstatically like fanatical fetish worshippers, who strain their words and their limbs all the more, the less they believe in the idols before which they dance". [*Conversations with Kafka*—Gustav Janouch, p. 56].

He does not merely fumble through the dark with dream-laden eyes and raise a scream of prayer to the absent or dead God each time his outstretched palms get burnt. He realises the true nature of human destiny, the collective destiny of human misery, the untold record of pain throughout history through a mature awareness of our fate:

> And as you go in the dazzling sun
> to feel with sad bewilderment

how all of life and its suffering
is in this steady following
a wall with jagged bottle or its rim.

(Eugenio Montale)

Against the elitist approach to the problem of 'I' and 'thou' or the writer's 'ego' verses community, modern art and literature assumes a measure of built-in involvement with 'other selves' and the community. The modern poet feels this identification almost intuitively. It is no longer Rimbaud's first person singular becoming the other and coming back to it. It is, on the other hand, an expanded awareness of the 'self', an ever-widening circle of consciousness where it contains in itself the farthest star.

The human spirit is not a prisoner of history and the continuity of human culture and civilisation is a standing testimony to man's continuing obsession with the harvest, falsifying and bewildering all the prophets of doom. The destiny of man is, no doubt, inseparable from the struggle for liberation of the human spirit in historical terms.

But each historical period assumes a prevailing system of values, a mode of aesthetic judgement and certain given moral standards, all of which may not be acceptable to the developed sensibility of a writer. Basically, art is a defence against dehumanisation and, to that extent, it calls us back to certain eternal values of life and love.

Literature, like any other creative art, assumes the temporality of human life and its being subject to the flux of time. This, however, need not lead us to a sense of despair, angst or rootlessness. What is important is to realise the possibility of creative delight in experience and to assert, almost against the whole range of myth-makers and media-managers of modern society, the supremacy, uniqueness and communal character of shared experience.

All art that is truly and authentically individual is also at the same time, poignantly universal. The microcosm reflects the destiny of the macrocosm. For experience always implies the possibility of the 'other'. To experience is to deny the loneliness of the 'self' and assert the existence of the 'other'. Once we deny the creative delight in experience, we are threatened by inanimate matter and the immensity of the physical world. Sartre's hero gets the feeling of nausea when he feels that he is almost being submerged by the hostile and strange look of the greedy, mechanistic and physical world around him. He has become 'alone' without realising it. He has broken up the bridges and connections with 'otherselves'.

The denial of the reality and even the validity of experience perhaps becomes a cruel necessity when experience is no longer a delight but has turned into a frightening nightmare. The world we live in has seen a number of such nightmarers. This has led either to a turning back on experience itself or to a withdrawal more and more into the windowless monad of the individual self.

Experience is, after all, another name for 'reality' and as Williams asserts in the poem "An Ordinary Evening in New Haven":

> We seek
> Nothing beyond reality; within it
> Everything, the spirit's alchemicana
> Included, the spirit that goes round about
> And though included, not merely the visible
> The solid, but the movable, the moment,
> The coming of the feasts and the habits
> The patterns of the heavens, high, night air.

The failure of the existentialism of the west is this inability to give a valid meaning to experience of the individual in relation to society. It is here that the poetry and art of the primitive people can have a lesson for us. There can be few primitive people, for example, as backward and as poor as the Kondhs living in the high hills and dense jungles of Orissa. The Kondh's life is full of misery from his birth:

> The pumpkin plant's tragedy is from the day.
> Two leaves shoot forth from the seed:
> Men pluck them out
> Man's tragedy is alike:

From childhood
Useless iron is thrown into corners
The poor man enters the forest
Crow-bar on the shoulders
Basket on the head
And life, only a tragic song.
(A Kondh song)

But tragedy is often endured with a smile. And at the end of all pain and misery there is thankfulness for the very fact of being alive. As in this Kondh song of an old man on the day of *Paus Purnima* festival:

The old hearts still beat
And we are alive
Here in this ancient village
Or dead ancestors
And so today we could partake
Of this great jubilation.

The simultaneous celebration and rejection of the world by the simple primitives can perhaps have a lesson for us,

And how similar is this to Dylan Thomas' statement:

"And the poem becomes, at last, the affirmation of the beautiful and terrible worth of the Earth. It grows into a praise of what is and what could be on this lump in the skies".

Man becomes not a windowless monad of the isolated self, and island but a complex web of relationships which define him and articulate his destiny.

True art today has to re-affirm the validity of human experience as the touchstone of culture and civilisation. Even when the experience is a nightmare, tragic or unbelievably sad, it will be that sad experience that will define our common human fate. Commitment to creative experience in literature and art is not merely a kind of vague social philosophy or political ideology. Commitment in literature is not the narrow preoccupation of any ideology of art. It is today the necessary premise that can bring together tradition and freedom, and the elite and the masses without surrendering to various forms of bondage. Indeed today it is the very condition of the survival of art and human civilisation.

# 16 | Meeting of Cultures: East and West

THE EAST is East, the West is West and the twain shall never meet. Perhaps there has never been a greater misjudgement based on a myopic, distorted vision and a lack of understanding of history. For despite the obvious differences in social and cultural evolution, political and economic institutions, attitudes and value-systems the East and the West have remarkably converged on many planes and in a host of complex and interrelated linkages throughout history. Pitirim Sorokin has painstakingly documented a large corpus of cultural, civilisational parallels in the dynamics of their evolution. It is only appropriate that we remember and emphasise these meeting points and common grounds, these parallels and similarities when we think of one of the greatest figures in contemporary culture who emphasised the universality of man, his common heritage and destiny. Romain Rolland, both in his life and letters intensely believed in man's unique essence despite superficial differences imposed by social, political and economic conditionings. For him the East and the West had ever acted and reacted on each other, mingled and coalesced even while retaining their unique identities.

Most of us are familiar with the usual binary oppositions posited by cultural historians between the East and the West. We have been told the East is instinctive, emotional, feminine in its langour, laziness and elegance; other—worldly, mystical, religious, mythical, superstitious, world-denying, anti-historical, obsessed with personal salvation and time as eternity, and with the hereafter and the beyond. The West, by contrast, we are told, is cognitive, rational, masculine in its energy and pragmatism, historical, emphasising the here and the now, obsessed with this world and what it offers and denying anything beyond it and beyond the body.

But these stereotypes of differences are somewhat superficial. If rationalism and Descartes' "I think, therefore I am" gave us modern science, the latter has brought us by now to the very depths of mystery and a realisation of the inadequacy of the merely rational. We have now to contend with holes in space, of the new frontiers of mind and the metaphysics of the material. This is not to mention the emphasis on the irrational or supra-rational by poets like Rimbaud or Baudelaire or philosophers like Nietzsche. Science and spirituality, rationalism and mysticism no longer look like north pole and south pole. We have now greater uncertainties in science which once held out a dream of total certainty and verifiable truth. And a scientist Miroslav Holub looks at a cell under the microscope and discovers word-less poetry that illumines our understanding of ourselves and the world. The West has always sought to go beyond the merely rational just as the East has also sought to find the roots of reason and relevance in emotion and instinct.

And Time is not always measured out in cofee-spoons in the West. Time is eternity and eternity is only the infatuation with the moment that holds us in its grip. It is not the continuous flow of ages or aeons. There is the story of a 14th century Belgian monastery to which came a youngman seeking know-ledge. He asked the ageing head of the monastery as to how they were not bored with nothing to do in a small isolated spot. The head pointed out to him a bird of beautiful golden plum-mage sitting on the branch of a nearby tree and the youngman was overwhelmed by this piece of beauty. The bird kept flying away from one tree to another and he kept looking at it and pursuing it. At last when he thought it was getting late he turned back and came to the monastery. He was astonished to see everything there changed and another head in charge. As if in answer to his sense of wonder someone brought him a mirror and looking at it he discovered to his dismay that he had lost half his teeth and the hair on his head was all grey. Then the head of the monastery told him: My dear boy, if it took you forty years to look at a bird without tiring and without being conscious of the passage of time why should we be bored in loneliness? There is a parallel story in Indian mythology which André Malraux refers to in his *Anti-Memoir*: Of Vishnu asking Narada the sage to fetch him a pail of water and Narada falling in love, marrying, raising a family and finally in a deluge losing all of them and suddenly hearing Vishnu's voice 'I am still waiting for you Narada with my unquenched thirst to get me a pail of water.'!

The East has generally not allowed any philosophic significance to history. It has been preoccupied with Being and history, by definition, is the Created becoming and hence only a form of Non-Being. But the East also examined the meaning of historicity and the tool for such analysis was what Western philosophy calls 'being in the world' or 'being in a situation' in the manner of Sartre and the existentialists. Yoga, Vedanta and Buddhism—as Mircea Eliade points out in his *Myths, Dreams and Mysteries*—all emphasise the essential and inevitable relativity of everything and therefore the non-reality of every situation and all conditions. And as he concludes "many centuries before Heidegger, Indian thought had identified in temporarity the fated dimension of all existence, just as it had foreseen, before Marx or Freud, the multiple conditioning of all human experience."

It is true the East and the West have viewed Death differently. Death was a definitive end, a finality, a state from which there was no return. The West looked upon Death that way and tried to overcome the anxiety it created by insulating it from day-to-day living. Slowly it became a dirty word, something to be forgotten, to be kept away in lonely oldage homes, hospital corridors or equally lonely homes. It was neither a new beginning as Eastern religions emphasised nor a mere stage in the process of living. When a person died he was to be bathed, anointed and sent away with precisely those things that he loved in life. For was he not beginning a new journey only? And the ancients, the dead ancestors had a role to play in the world of the living. They were propitiated, offerings were made to them. Thus for the East Death was not nothingness, nor an abyss or a blank wall. It was neither definitive nor absurd. Seen in Eastern perspective it was homologous with the dialectical moment of the discovery of the final illusory character of everything or *Maya*. For non-existence was only a mode of perceiving the Void. Buddhism went further to assert it as *nirvana*, as release from the ever-recurring cycle of life. Death was only an opportunity to take us nearer to this final release by enabling yet another lease to time in which to work towards that end.

Despite the general Western attitude of anxiety and absurdity towards Death in its more obvious manifestations, there have been many writers, poets and authors who have looked upon Death as a part of becoming and a step towards the renewal of existence and not as an abrupt end. In the poetry of Rilke and Lorca, of Eliot and Yeats one can discover a more complex attitude towards Death and an awareness of its redemptive and extending role. It extends existence, opens up a window on unexplained mystery and through that adds yet another complex dimension to life.

Thus in the two broad areas of Time and Death the West and the East have sought to understand and learn from each other's attitude and values. Time for the Western man is as complex and as interwoven with the reality and shadows of life as for the Eastern man. Time is both eternity and the moment. Its transience is reflected in life that makes it so charming, lovable and adorable. We love it, hold it in our palm, are even obsessed with it precisely because it is so evanescent, so ephemeral. And man is not fragmented by Time or Death. Both these phenomena only add a lovable dimension to life in the perception of their duality.

On the other hand the Eastern world is not other-worldly. It too believes in the here and the now. It too believes in the primacy of the person and the moment, the ultimate relevance of the moment and the significance of relationship, the I and Thou matrix. It denies and affirms life simultaneously. Both in the East and the West our art, poetry and literature have emphasised the other dimension of creativity: that man is engaged in a culpable rivalry with god and art is one of our fundamental defences against Death and decay. That art is what time does to man and the Word is our ultimate weapon against death and dissolution.

The Protestant ethic may have been the moving spirit behind

capitalism and Western sociologists may still relate the low growth-rate in the East to the absence of an acquisitive instinct but that way are we not moving towards a greater appreciation of the negative points of affluence and poverty? It may be simplistic to talk of the life we have lost in living or the wisdom we have lost in knowledge but now we increasingly realise both in the West and the East that the machine can relieve us of drudgery but it cannot live for us. The awareness is dawning, faced by ecological disaster, urban decay, threat of war and de-humanisation on one side and the grinding poverty and empty stomachs on the other, that the East and West not only have often met but that more than ever before they must meet now halfway. That way we can marry the city to the jungle, the noise and information explosion to silence and the still centre of Being, the instinct and imagination to cognition and reason; and above all the joy of living and celebration of life to the pessimistic hollowness threatening to engulf us all.

# 17 Epic and Romance: The Archetypal Relation between Narrative and Destiny

EPIC IS perhaps narration at its most exalted and dignified form. Here the narrative form is apparently complex but it is a complexity that incorporates and conceals a profound simplicity. The complexity emerges out of the myriads of events, of plots and sub-plots, of tales of grandeur and greatness, of great battles of the human spirit, of the destiny of man and of men in society. They are intricately woven and warmly in folded and as they unweave one is face to face with life itself—with all its harshness and beauty. But underlying this complexity there is a simple pattern, a moving, connecting pattern that gives the events their meaning and significance.

Epic is narration but so too is life. A narration of events, of happenings from which in the short span of time that is allotted to us in this world we try to seek out some purpose, some meaning. Is life a narration of a given theme as pera pre-determined pattern or is it a report which we prepare to be submitted to someone who has sent us here? When events are too much for us, when despite all efforts we fail to comprehend and control them, when enmeshed in our unmeaning and helplessness we are tempted to point an accusing finger at an absent God, somewhere over there, a minor epic gets composed. When we feel we perhaps have just got a glimpse of the essential reality, of the meaning that underlies the events, of the days and nights that pass over us like flowing water on a stone and yet the meaning still eludes us; when we have an intimation that something for sure is in the clouds but it is not for us, when we have to negotiate with the world and its total disregard and indifference, the romance inherent in the epic gets enacted. When the residence of all our dreams looks like a wistful cloud that floats on to nowhere, when the dazzling impermanence of our days besets us and we beg our meanings from them and their frayed loveliness and tragic beauty the essential romantic mode is again and again brought home to us.

In an epic the story does not end. In a true sense in its end is its beginning, as in our lives. And the romance in the epic is inherent in the enactment of destiny. It is the ultimate romantic mode, the perception of love and passion in their dazzling beauty and elegance. Here love is the Being in its most vivid state and passion is what ignites the events, the moments and the lives of the protagonists, the heroes as also the anti-heroes. And love is not ordinary love. It is a mode of self-discovery, as much as the ultimate knowledge of the other. It is a sob in the blood stream and in each living cell and at the same time it is poetry that partakes of culture heavy with our instinct. It is a shadow in Plato's cave and at the same time an arduous path to God. It combines anxiety and intimacy, the ultimate thrill and the ever-immanent regression.

In fact Epic is Romance, the ultimate narrative in the romantic mode, capable of acquiring meanings with changing times and social values. The same is true for Homer's Ulysses as much as Vyasa's Mahabharata or Valmiki's Ramayana. Ulysses sailing into the high seas in Homer comes back to Ithaca to become a man of this world. Its here and now claim him. Its sun-laden promise and its myriad temptations hold him in their trap. But not so in case of Dante's Ulysses whose restless, peaceless soul goes on seeking the strange and the unknown beyond the known seas, and with his dear friends till the 'earthly heaven' has been sighted, across the blinding waves, on the horizon. And there is the end to his search for meaning, for significance without finally arriving anywhere. The turbulent journey is itself the meaning. The Europe of 14th century and its world view peeps out of Dante just as that of classical Greece does in Homer. And in Nikos Kazantzakis Ulysses is the modern man: in his delectable and tragic combination of explosive ambition and terrible despair. The Ulysses of Dante and Kazantzakis are miles away from the socially suave and the ultimately life-accepting protagonist of Homer. In the former authors he is a strange amalgam of revolt and despair, of blinding passion and merciless pessimism. In Ezra Pound's *Cantos* and Eliot's *Wasteland* it is yet another Ulysses incarnation. Tiresias seeking to encompass the new futilities and the new darknesses of a darkened age. But perhaps Joyce's Ulysses is the most unusual, starting his perception in the funeral procession of Glasenvin and the burial. Ulysses is now Bloom of Dublin face to face with a new Hell. And perhaps it is not just for a season. Perhaps it is for an eternity that will enter and live in the soul as the ultimate love, the ultimate destiny.

And so too in the Mahabharata. The most knowledgeable and the wise have to commit the gravest follies. The Dice game would become an act of tearing the soul and the beginning of the apocalypse. The drum beats of a fratricidal war sound in the minor nuances of envy and deceit that are the hall-mark of life and its blindfolded journey. What do those wisemen do to hold back events? The Bhisma Pitamahas, the Dronacharyas, the Kripacharyas et al? The all-knowing, all-seeing Vasudeva has to pretend helplessness for it is after all the play of destiny over which no one, himself included, has control. And what tales of passion and romance? Of Amba for Bhisma that leads to endless penance, through myriad births and deaths to avenge the rejection and the ultimate humiliation that a woman can face. And even while knowing and realising the validity of the ground of the sacral word for Bhisma to be finally in the battle of Kurukshetra to work out the destiny consigning oneself to the ordained bed of arrows and choosing death only when the sun returns on the south-bound journey. And the interplay of passions that finally blends the stories of a blind Dhritarastra, a cursed Pandu, a tragic, alienated Karna seething with the remorse of complete rejection and the endless pathos of an unanswered question who am I.

Yes, destiny is the theme of the narration in the epic and destiny is the ultimate in the romantic mode. In fact it is the only theme, which as it unweaves, throws up hundreds of subthemes, plots and sub-plots, each delicately linked to the other but finally subserving only to illustrate the play of destiny. In that view of things an epic is finally the tale of romance, of tragedy and grandeur, of love and passion blinding in their effulgence and energy against the ultimate backdrop of destiny.

And is there any fulfilment for any of the protagonists? As they fall, one after the other, in the *Mahayatra* after the battle of Kurukshetra, we know what they craved for, what they thought they missed or life denied them. The King of Dharma who had pawned away his wife in the Dice game has the question tearing at his soul: did she, did Draupadi really love him as much as she loved Bhima? And Draupadi has the feeling that perhaps Partha never loved her as much as he loved his friend Krishna. Everyone is unfulfilled, everyone has lost at the end of the war, when there is only a pervading emptiness, a howl of silence and anguish in the soul, an engulfing darkness in the midst of which no lights can shine. The sight of the hell that is Dharmaraja's destiny is indeed everyone's—enmeshed in ignorance, unknowing and a helpless waiting, in dread and shivering.

The Epic is narrative at its ultimate, at its grandest. And yet don't they tend to illustrate a bitter truth; there is so little after all to say and so much time to say it in? For the end is known, the final charm, the ultimate romance of the circular end is destined. It is only the weaving, the hungry spider's weaving of the web that is oddly and tragically beautiful in its desolation. The lesson is there—the final love and loss that belongs, as the dust settles and the drums are silenced, once again to the wind, the shivering dying grass and the dead seed cones. Only an impatient Krishna would await the final arrow for the departure from this play on earth. Guilt-ridden, desolate, anguished he awaits Jara's quivering arrow to be unleashed as the last act of romance and love. For love is passion, is death, is destiny and the epic's strength of narrative capacity is finally in this romantic mode of discovering unmeaning even while looking for meaning and significance.

The 'concrete universal' that Ransom speaks of following Hegel is perhaps this: the epic's universal of man's acre, the human predicament wrought like the spider's web in the romantic mode. As Wimsatt would say "if a work of literature is not in a simple sense either more individual or more universal than other kinds of writing it may yet be such an individual or such a complex of meaning that it has a special relation to the world of universals."

This *special relation* is perhaps the archetypal relation between the narrative and destiny, between romance and tragic passion.

# 18 Modern Science and Primitive Ritual: The Need for Reconciliation

ANY TRADITIONAL society undergoing rapid transformation throws up several problems having a bearing on the personality-structure of the individual and its social hierarchy. Value systems undergo rapid transformation in such a situation of flux. Science and its hand-made technology are secular in their impact. The changes brought about in the socio-economic structure and the individual's approach to reality are linked to the process by which 'profane' technology and 'sacred' ritual are sought to be married. This article makes an attempt to look at this process of reconciliation with reference to the Santal community particularly in north Orissa. The first part of the article discusses the general proposition of the confrontation between primitive ritual and modern technology. In the second part, an attempt is made to see the operation of this confrontation in one particular area of social activity, namely, the modernisation of agriculture.

## I

The erosion of the belief in rituals is linked to the awakening and intensification of a spirit of rationalism. Rituals depend upon an intuitive perception of reality by a mind attuned to such perception and an implicit faith in the efficacy of the activities associated with the ritual for solution of the life-crises. The foundation of such belief is an unquestioning faith that accepts things either because they have been handed down from posterity and are, therefore, sanctified by tradition or because non-deservance of them is taboo. Rationalism impinges on this kind of unquestioning faith and starts asking disturbing questions. It is not satisfied by explanations readily offered. It would like to go beyond simple answers. Technology is the product and the expression of a temper based on such a logical frame of mind and is thus, in a way, directly inimical to primitive ritual. The confrontation between these two frames of mind, the two mental climates as they were, is evident in several fields of economic activity and societal relations such as agricultural operations, attitude towards sickness, diseases, and death, divinations and the supernatural, approach to medicine, political and social leadership and, above all, in attitudes towards life and death. The confrontation is not merely in the mind of the individuals in Santal society. It has a social significance whose importance cannot be under-estimated. Such confrontations are universal in culture undergoing rapid transformation when inherited tradition comes face to face with the modern tamper, the new approaches to reality.

Such confrontation has a relevance for modernisation and development. Sometimes an entire village is face to face with such opposing forces. "When a village is faced with a suggestion of change, there exists a balance of forces. On one side of the scales are these forces which are against change-conservatism, apathy, fear and the like; on the other side are the forces for change—dissatisfaction with existing conditions, village pride, and so on. Successful community development consists largely of choosing these projects, where the balance is almost even, and then trying to lighten the forces against change or to increase the factors making for change." (Jackson, 1956: 30).

The art and science of development consist in discovering the modalities of bringing about an optimal balance between them or making the forces of tradition and heritage strengthen, through a well-conceived and well-directed process of reinterpretation of the tradition, the forces conductive to change, modernisation and economic growth. Lucy Mair suggests as a generalization of wide application that "the conservative force of tradition is never proof against the attraction of economic advantage, provided that the advantage is sufficient and is clearly recognised. In the case of land it is abundantly clear that the emotional and religious attitudes towards it which are inculcated by native tradition have not prevented the development of commercial attitude". (Mair, 1957:52)

The relationship between myth and rituals on one hand, and their relationships to personality and social structure have been variously studied by anthropologists. Monica Wilson, for example, emphasises the relevances of rituals to values of the group. "Rituals reveal values at their deepest level . . . . man expresses in ritual what moves them most, and since the form of expression is conventionalized and derivative, it is the value of the group that are revealed. I see in the study of rituals the key to an understanding of the essential constitution of human societies." (Monica Wilson, 1954). Kirk connected them to two primary functions both of which had socialisation as their objective. "Apart from routine acts of propitiation and sacrifice rituals tend to be either *rites de passage* or connected with agrarian fertility. The continuation of social and natural regularity in more general ways accounts for other types (of rituals)". (Kirk, 1971)

The Studies undertaken among three tribal groups in north Orissa by this author reveal an interesting connection between three types of hierarchies. Economic and political power hierarchy have generally gone together. The more affluent in society have also got access to political power and are able to manipulate this power for furthering their economic gains. Thus there is a growing close nexus between political hierarchy and economic status. Socio-ritual status, however, is more often in a situation of confrontation with these two different status-symbols.

The confrontation of technology and rituals has to be viewed in this wider context of social and political factors, for in the Santal mind technology and the new politics are always associated as integral to each other. Since Independence there has been very little industrialisation in the Mayurbhanj district. This is perhaps the reason why the Santal has been less influenced by the impact of the industrial world than the Mundas and Oraons who inhabit the neighbouring district of Sundergarh. Mayurbhanj does not have a modern industrial city comparable to the steel city of Rourkela. Nor does it has the more developed labour and mining areas as at Birmitrapur or around Rajgangpur in Sundergarh district. While the Mundas and Oraons have come under the more disturbing impact of urbanisation and industrialisation, their resistance to the new change is not as strong as that of the Santal. This is perhaps because the Mundas as also the Oraons are not as conscious of a glorious Great Tradition on which the Santal lays so much emphasis. The nature of confrontation between technology and ritual has thus a qualitative difference in the two areas, namely, the Santal-dominated Mayurbhanj district and the Munda and Oraon dominated Sundergarh district.

The Santal ethos in Sumner's sense of "some of the characteristics, usages, insights standards and codes by which a group is differentiated and individualised in character from other groups", is a very well formed echoes. It enabled him to take a fairly rational approach to the growing technology that invades his life today. But the capacity to pinpoint the impediments to the modernisation process is sadly lacking. The economic benefits of the process is gradually becoming clearer but even here also ambivalance remains, at least on two counts. Firstly, whether the agency that ushers in the benefit, namely the new political institutions are to be looked upon as intrusions and resisted or welcomed; whether participation in them should be total and enthusiastic or one should withdraw. Secondly, whether the new modes of leadership devoid of folklore and mythology should be accepted or the traditional leadership should continue to hold sway and command allegiance and loyalty. On the other hand, and because of this ambivalence, the so-called ritual basis of society and the Great Tradition have neither been fully accepted nor acted upon by the rank and file. Thus neither the new technology and its ally the new political system and the leadership nor the traditional ritual and the leadership based on it has been able to bring about the very necessary reapprochment or reconciliation between the two opposing value-systems and forms of socio-economic organisation. Basically socio-cultural development and a new renaissance of economic growth and flowering of autonomous culture demand the capacity for corporate action and individual dedication. Neither of these determinants seem to be very much in sight.

Like most under-developed societies, the Santal society shows a typical inability to maintain an organisation. The capacity of a culture to maintain an organisation depends on its related capacity of social synthesising and bringing together a large number of social values to the level of community participation. The incompatabilities between particular aspects of a culture which impede corporate action are precisely those conditions that impede modernisation. The new technology is based upon what Banfield calls "the ethos of a moral familism". As he observes "We are apt to take it for granted that economic and political associations will arise whenever technical conditions and natural resources permit. If the state of the technical art is such that large gains are possible by conserting the activities of many people then organising skill will appear from somewhere, organisations will spring up and grow. This assumption is wrong because it overlooks the crucial importance of culture". (Benfield, 1968)

Modernisation has its impact on the ritual-based social structure of the Santal world in several dimensions. The most important area of interaction between tradition and ritual has been the pattern of leadership. Political change in a traditional society comes slowly but it tends to affect almost all aspects of community life. The approach to life and death, to pleasure and pain, to self and the others, flow from certain given systems of value. These value systems are part of the cultural orientation of the community and are often deeply enshrined in the personality structure. The value systems in their turn are linked to a host of socio-economic factors, tradition and mythology, approach to disease and death, the viewpoint on the natural and the supernatural and the nature and role of political changes.

The new political system which is alike to the new technology has not been able to throw up this capacity for corporate action. On the other hand, it has only resulted in either distorting or killing the earlier forms of corporate action in socio-cultural matters. This is a problem that has to be tackled at many levels so that the new technology and old rituals are brought together or nearer with a view to formulate patterns of human cooperation that would make corporate action both for economic development and cultural autonomy possible.

The confrontation of technology and ritual is not a simplistic factor. After all a technological system also tends to develop its own rituals. But ritual in the traditional religious-cultural sense implies a host of symbolic functions which are kept outside the realm of logic and rationalism. The technological world, on the other hand, calls for less and less of intuition and more of reason, an ability to analyse and co-ordinate details rather than to take an intuitive world view. In his foreword to Paulo Freire's *Padagogy of The Oppressed.* Richard Shaull referred to the "paradoxical dual role of the new technology which according to him holds a hope for the future. Our advanced technological society is rapidly making objects of most of us and subtly programming us into confermity to the logic of its system. To the degree that this happens, we are also becoming submerged in a new 'culture of silence'.

The paradox is that the same technology which does this to us also creates a new sensitivity to what is happening. Especially among young people, the media together with the erosion of old concepts of authority open the way to acute awareness of this new bondage". (Richard Shaull,1972)

The new political system and the new technology in the field of agriculture, medicine, education and economic development therefore bring in value-systems and attitudes which are in direct conflict with the ritual-based puristic approach to life and reality. Technology also is secular in its impact just like political democracy or the Panchayati Raj.

## II

Technology is not merely a matter of tools and equipment; it implies a particular intellectual and emotive structure, and a social environment with specific value-systems which in their turn, determine the personality-structure and its approach to technology. All technological changes and innovations, therefore, presuppose specific cultural determinations. Innovation of techniques, their diffusion, acceptance and proper utilisation are all linked to sociological questions—the structures of society and its values and the personality-structure.

Take, for example, modernisation of agriculture, which implies a growing complexity of intercultural operations. Seed has to be sown at a particular time, the application of fertilisers, weeding, hoeing, etc. have also to be at specific, prescribed time. In other words, the agriculturist has to discipline his mind to the needs of the time-sequence, the phasing, the duration. Leisurely, 'let do' activity will not do. He has to become to an extent a slave to the clock. Lewis Mumford, in his "Technics and Civilisation" rightly stated that the time-piece and not the steam-engine was the real father of the Industrial Revolution.

For the Santal cultivator, this acceptance of the tyranny of the clock has been slow and difficult. Given the cultural basis of Santal society and Santal personality, it is difficult for the Santal to accept the discipline of time; the Santal is rarely bothered about time and its flux. I know of instances when five Santal will spend a whole day draining out water from a pool to catch ultimately a quarter kilogram of fish just because one of them sighted one medium-sized fish in it. A whole village may spend a whole day running curiously after a wounded pigeon limping and hopping away from one tree to another, hoping to catch it when it falls dead. This may be what Huizinga in his "Decline of the Middle Ages" calls the play-element in culture; his thesis being that man is basically a player, a *homo ludens*.

A number of social festivals and the accompanying communal worships are directly linked to agricultural operations. These are primarily:

1. *Erok or Eroh* (worship at the time of sowing seeds)
2. *Sura Sagen Mahmane* (when the crop is slowly growing)
3. *Asadia and Helhed* (de-weeding operations)
4. *Jom Nowa* (worship to Jaher era with the new crop)

Besides these, during *Mhga* and *Baha* festivals, in worshipping the Jaher era, the invocations are for "good heavy monsoon, the earth filling up with flowers, fruits and everywhere green crops coming".

The festivals are thus partly 'vegetation' ceremony and partly 'fecundity' ceremony. The invocations (Murmu, 1967) are reminiscent of Vedic prayers for plenty and peace. But there is always the feeling that much is left to the operation of the good will of the gods or *Bongas*. After all they will finally determine the quality of the harvest and nothing human beings do will really change the picture.

On the contrary, if they are not properly worshipped or they are not pleased, or if for some reason we invite their wrath then there will be poor crop or even large-scale failure of crop. This author has been surprised by the lazy and complacent attitude which many cultivators in Santal villages exhibit when it comes to productivity in their field, good crop or the need for ensuring proper cropping condition. This attitude is variously expressed. Sometimes directly, sometimes even by insinuations. But it becomes clear that they are learning only slowly from non-tribals, particularly the Mahatos in their own village who are very good cultivators and who do not care very much for extra-rational forces of *Bongas* or gods and goddesses. The Santal's belief that good crops are the result of proper propitiation of the gods and goddesses and bad crops or crop failure is due to their wrath is deeply entrenched in the social value-system and personality. The rationalistic approach to the subject—the need for proper ploughing, proper inputs, seeds, fertilizer, application of pesticides in time, proper and timely irrigation is slowly coming in but a sense of their urgency, immediacy and relevance are diluted by these extra-rational factors. For example, in a village an old man told this author that the Eroh festival was not properly done and the crops started dying in September and there was not even a drop of rain from the sky and not even a cloud was sighted. "They tried to save the crop by bringing a pump that made lots of noise and the little water in the village tank was used up. Still there was no rain and the standing peddy crop finally died. Could they save it? No. How can they when Jaher Era wanted it the other way about", he asked.

Belief in propitiating gods and goddesses beginning certain agricultural operations by relevant worships sometimes effects agriculture adversely in another way. One Santal village had, after lot of extension work and persuasion, taken to hybrid maize. The fields were properly cultivated. The crop was coming up very well. But the *Asadia* festival was delayed. The villager *Manjhi* had gone to his father-in-law's house where he lay very sick. He had not been able to decide, in consultation with the village elder, the date for *Asadia* and, as such, the festival had not been held. And nobody in the village would enter the field for de-weeding as *Asadia* worship had not been done and it was a taboo to do so. Some young boys who had read up to ninth and tenth class found that the weeds had grown very fast and the fine maize crop was going to be stunted and smothered unless de-weeding was immediately done. They were described as 'faithless' and finally the voice of the elders won. The de-weeding was done only after *Asadia*, but more than a forthnight's delay considerably damaged the crop.

## REFERENCES

Banfield, E.C.: (1968) *The Moral Basis of a Backward Society*, The Free Press. (Research Centre in Economic Development and Cultural Change, University of Chicago) p. 8.

Jackson, I.C.: (1956) *Advance in Africa: A Study of Community Development in Eastern Nigeria*, London, Oxford University Press.

Kirk, G. S.; (1971) *Myth: Meaning and Functions in Ancient and Other Cultures*, Cambridge University Press, p. 19.

Mair, Lucy P. : (1957) *Studies in Applied Anthropology*, London School of Economics, Monography on Social Anthropology No. 16, London. University of London, Athlone Press.

Murmu, Raghunath: (1967) *Bakhens*, (In Santali Language and 01 script).

Shaule, Richard: (1972) Forewod to Paule Freire's *Padagogy of the Oppressed*, Penguin. 1972, p. 13.

# 19 | Convergence and Complementarity: Science in Post-Modern Society

THE SCIENTIFIC spirit is as old as the emergence of the first man on this planet. Man's curiosity has made him ask questions and seek answers to them. The phenomena in nature, rains, thunder, lightning, earthquake, volcanic eruptions, the changing seasons, the waxing and waning of light, the birth and death of the living—all of them have made him wonder about the 'why' and 'how' of the events. He has looked at the sky and wondered at the myriad beads of light sparkling in the clear sky, the moon changing itself everyday each fortnight. The questions have turned inside to his own feelings and emotions: of love, anger, anguish, disgust; to his cognition, knowledge, remembering and forgetting, to the pattern of life from the cradle to the grave; to his dreams and imagination, his fantasies, fears and myth-makings. It has also turned to the web of togetherness with others in society, the eternal binary complementarity—confrontation between I and thou. Sometimes he has felt desperately lonely, helplessly looking for friends, and companionship, persons to he can communicate his feelings, his desires, his tragedies and triumphs and with whom he can share the inner life of the self. At other times he has got fed up with 'those others' and has craved how to get away from them, and this world. This innate contradictory feeling within him is as old as his existence on the planet. Sartre only summed it up in two opposing statements: 'hell is the self'; 'hell is other people'.

Questions are eternal to man. In his individual life it dies only with his death. In the life of human civilization it will remain till man remains on this planet.

And so science is coeval with society. The scientist in primitive society had his discoveries, his inventions. He invented fire—perhaps the most revolutionary invention of man; he invented housing, from cave to all varieties of makeshift enclosed space on branches of trees and autonomous 'constructions'; of clothing and jewellery, the tree-barks and stone beads; and patterns of singing, dancing, living and celebrating life and death, of the intricacy of rituals dedicated to gods, seasons and life itself. At one stage may be the village barber was the village surgeon. In Aristotle physics and metaphysics went together as much as modern day space science and linguistics.

Man sought to discover, to invent. He also lived his life, in himself and with others. His life-style was the hall-mark of his society. Its arts, artefacts and fabrications, its songs and poems, its mythologies and philosophy, its dances and paintings. They defined his culture, his overall life-style. Intuitive knowledge, imagination, fantasies went into the making of all these—be it a poem, a painting, a song, a dance or an object of aesthetic beauty. Cognition, knowledge and techniques were also necessary for bringing them into life. But they were peripheral along with the capacity to organise and to manage. He also had his faith, his gods, his beliefs, his religious litanies, his *mantras*, his spells and charms and so on.

Scientific discovery on the other hand demanded rigorous logic, intense reasoning cognitive knowledge, the organisation of rational thought and de-linking one's subjective feelings, faiths and beliefs from them. Objectivity, cold reasoning, merciless scrutinising, a questioning mind and the capacity to link together ideas, discover the connections between objects and ideas—these became the *sine qua non* of the scientific spirit.

Modern science which is supposed to be the distinguishing hall-mark of modern society is generally looked upon as a Post-Renaissance phenomenon. It is linked to the waning of the Middle Ages and the emergence of Renaissance which emphasised qualities like uniqueness, originality and putting one's name on stone. Jacob Burckhardt raised the question as to when and how 'the modern' era began and approvingly quoted Benjamin Nelson's formulation in this regard that the Renaissance symbolised new 'structures, of consciousness'. In this new structure Descartes' *cogito ergo sum*, 'I think, therefore I am' formed the centrepiece and even while some dogmas still remained thc 'critical logics of casuistry and conscience' which emphasised an individual interpretation gained supremacy.

This was also linked sociologically to the explosive French Revolution, the emergence of what was believed to be a new religion of man which emphasised his basic humanity as opposed to the supremacy of traditional faiths.

The invention of the steam-engine and the revolution in the technique and technology of the production process (and, as a consequence, of production-relations) marked yet another phase of the 'modern'. The drudgery of man's labour versus the inanimate world was to give place to the new agency, the machine, the handmaid of technology, the latter itself being a product of science and the modern spirit. This led to the idea and conviction in man's unlimited progress in every sphere and the dominance and spread of rationality in all areas of human endeavour.

These in turn led to the emergence of modernism in aesthetics and culture—the rise of the museums where, as Daniel Bell observes "cultural artefacts are wrenched from their traditional places and displayed in a new context of syncretism". Bell goes on to say: "history mixed up and consciousness jumbled, as when Nepoleon ransacked Egypt and Europe to stuff the Louvre with his trophies. Yet emperors have always displayed their power by placing their heads on coins and their heels on culture". There was also modernism in culture with its systematic assault on the ordered perceptions of space and time and evolving a syntax of disjunctive forms and an idiom of un-co-ordinated feelings. There was the endless experimentalism of the *avant-garde* that looked to the surreal, to the subconscious and the collective unconscious. There was the vigorous emphasis on the epistemological roots of aesthetic perceptions which found its ultimate expression in Kantian metaphysics: knowledge was not dependent on or derived from a *a priori*, pre-existing forms; it was the product of an activity of the individual consciousness.

Science was thus the most important hall-mark of the age that dawned on the decline of the Middle Ages. It was the age of rationalism, of liberal humanism, of the religion of man, of new art and aesthetics. It led to endless new inventions and discoveries in physical and material sciences, in earth sciences, in space sciences and life sciences. The microscope, the telescope, the fathoming of the depths of space and of the individual cell and the new knowledge of the universe, of man and of nature.

Modern technology came with modern science and what is called the industrial society was the product of the new technology. In the beginning it was an euphoria of progress, of unlimited growth, of man's conquest over nature and the end of human drudgery, deprivation, poverty and squalor. The new age of material well-being, control over the material world and nature had dawned. It was the new era of affluence, of the emergence of the 'leisured class' and the liberation of the human spirit to fulfil its creative urges to the fullest extent unburdened by lack of time and opportunities. Man was free to create and not go on wasting time to gather the minimum requisites of living and surviving.

In *Technics and Civilization*, Lewis Mumford proposed the hypothesis that it was not the steam-engine but the time-piece that was the true symbol of the modern. The time-piece symbolised the dominance of time over human impulse. Time was not only money. Time was life, was art, was at the core of economic development and growth of affluence. Man subjected himself to the dictates of time: in the agricultural farm and field by the needs of inter-cultural operations, on the shop floor of industries by the rhythm of the machine and of course in the more sophisticated business and trade practices. Time became the measure of development. Societies that did not bother about time remained poor. In the Third World the people had no regard for the value of time, it was argued. They can spend days together on merry making, on rituals, on festivals, on celebrations while economic activities held no attraction for them. That was the case, even in greater measure, with the tribal societies, the ethnic minorities in the Third World countries like India. An entire village can spend a whole day chasing a bird with bows and arrows; they can sing and dance for days on end in a seemingly never-ending festival. But the new philosophy of development demanded a subservience to the clock, to the time-piece.

The story of Industrial Revolution and the French Revolution and their complementarity in ushering in the modern world as we know it, is well known. Science was at the backdrop of both as also, howsoever indirectly, behind new and *avant-garde* art, the new aesthetic the new production processes and production relations and the emergence of the new industrialised, urbanised societies. First it was the blackened landscape of chimneys spouting smoke, the industrial worker with gin shops on the left and the right and social tensions. Then the growth of capitalism, the war-machine, the international competition for new markets, the mergence of imperialism and the two World Wars, the nuclear holocaust, the subsisting memory of Hiroshima and its aftermath—this is the history, at the most, of two hundred years.

Slowly but imperceptibly dreams turned into nightmares. The world had been looked upon by many as if it was a vast engine for progress and not a place that was to be made fit for man to live in peace with himself and with others. It took two World Wars and the nuclear holocaust to make man understand that science can be used to destroy man. It was no longer possible to feel comfortable by asserting the neutrality of science, its amorality and its role as a force both for good and evil depending upon the user and his will. The moral dimension of science, its ethical preoccupations were now increasingly talked about.

Was science a Frankentein, a monster that can destroy civilization? Was it drunk with its power and glory as the ultimate knowledge that had conquered nature, space and time? Was it afflicted by the disease of a *hubris* that was destined to bring about its own nemesis? Was science desperately in need of realising its social, moral and ethical responsibilities? Was it in need of humility, in need of recognising its limitations and its areas of grey and dark? For had nor the Owl of Minerva that flew at dusk now folded up its wings? Had not the Cartesian dictum 'I think, therefore I am' turned full circle: the explosion of knowledge and information that made it impossible for the individual human consciousness to understand and think for oneself and was, in helplessness and apathy, slowly surrendering the primacy of his 'own thinking' to that of the hidden persuaders that Vance Packand speaks of? And they could be hidden and not so hidden, the media-managers the opinion-modulators, the schemers of ideas and concepts. All those who not content with managing our political and economic systems would also like to order our lives and our thoughts.

Eliot had crystallised it in his anguished question: where is the life we have lost in living? Where is the knowledge we have lost in information? Where is the wisdom we have lost in knowledge? Yeats, before him, had spoken of the centre not being able to hold and the fragmentation of the spirit.

Secular ideologies had become stilted and nearly unmeaning. Technology, as an engine of progress, had become demonised by those who held the keys to industry, the war-machine and the profits. The independence and the authentic quest of the *avant-garde* in art had degenerated into superficialities and trivialities. All the gods had failed and man had to begin anew. The Hegelian alienation of 'spirit', the Marxian concept of productive alienation and the existential alienation that existentialists like Kierkegaard and Sartre spoke of had also come full circle. No scripture, no faith, no scientific doctrine, no given formula was adequate. On the other hand the individual consciousness was also not adequate. In fact it was too helpless, utterly inadequate to measure up to the challenge of the knowledge explosion. Man was almost saying: 'as for thinking, our machines can do that for us'. Man was once more utterly helpless. He was variously described and portrayed in the literature and arts of the last one and half centuries as the rootless, the estranged, the alienated, as one suffering from non-belonging. The direction of history had been lost. Collective destruction was a distinct, horrifying possibility. But the greater reality was the individual *ennui* and boredom, the lack of a zest for living, and the assertion of man's creative urge and the approaching death of the creative instinct.

No, science was not the only villain of the piece. It was not as if all this happened because of science. Science was amoral. Man had to use it optimally, appropriately. Science must have a human face, a human dimension. Science cannot disclaim totally its ethical and moral responsibilities. Science has to look more into the nature of man and his being in society than into the atom and outer space. Many and varied have been the critics of science and its role in what is being called loosely, the post-modern society and the role of ethics in it.

Modernisation and modernity were used as key words in political and social theories of the last nearly one century. Traditional societies of the Third World were to modernise, were to gear themselves up to meet the demands of economic growth and change. But suddenly the West had seen the empty face of modernity and scholars had started speaking of not only a post-Industrial society, the society that has gone through the future shock and is now face to face with itself, the third wave. Man is left unaided once more and has to find his own way.

Thinking people the world over have tried to speak of alternatives. They have drawn attention to the more obvious dichotomies that afflict human civilization today. It is not merely science that has to wear a human face, owning up its moral and ethical dimensions. It is not merely technology that must also be human and bring itself down to the human dimension. The whole business of development, triggered by science and technology has to concern itself with man's culture, his life-style, his essential humanity. The very first task in this scenario is to be humanising science and luckily the growth of science itself has led on to such a new mood of humility. It is the convergence of scientific enquiry and spirit and the faith of earlier centuries. It is not an accident but was perhaps inherent in the growth of science itself. Science today is face to face with myriad unresolved questions. Gone are the certainties of nineteenth century and even the first half of this century. When Einstein spoke of his feeling as "a child picking up pebbles at the shores of the infinite ocean" it was to an extent a sense of personal humility; but it was also a frightening but slowly-growing realisation that perhaps one can never know enough of Time and Space, that what is unknown will perhaps ever remain unknowable.

More and more science speaks of the edge of infinity, the black holes, the naked singularity and the concept of Space and Time being in crisis. More and more it has spoken of facing the unknowable in its futile attempt to look beyond the Infinite, to unravel the mystery of the creation of the Universe and its connection to Time as a concept. Paul Davies, the author of *The Edge of Infinity*, quotes St. Augustine approvingly: "the world was made with time and not in time". Liebnitz had given us a parallel argument, "either god created nothing at all or he created the world before any assignable time". Paul Davies, almost in tune with this line of argument says "Time came into existence with the Big Bang; so also causality for there is no causality outside Time".

Thus the concept of Time has gone through a revolutionary transformation from the days of Newtonian physics. And so too space. There is now a growing recognition that there are perhaps regions of space where gravity is so strong that it tends to overwhelm and swallow up everything—objects, structures, all physical laws. New discoveries tend to make scientists believe that uncontrolled gravity can twist space and time into destruction at what Paul Davies calls singularities. According to him a singularity is a weird non-place where space-time is ripped open and matters may enter or leave the physical universe, singularities, he holds, lie at the centre of the blackholes and mark the creation and destruction of the universe. At a singularity gravitational force can be infinite. On the edge of infinity bizarre effects occur—time is reversed, cause and effect breakdown, and matter is totally annihilated.

Such humility in the face of the unknowable was voiced by Einstein in 1927 in the Solvay Conference where most of the major originators of quantum theory were present, when he elucidated his thesis that quantum mechanics can at best be an incomplete description of physical reality. And to his dying day this remained a conviction with him.

Was it not at a deeper level a search for complementarity? Was it not a realisation that the physical may in some sense be also the repository of the metaphysical, that the inadequacy in our knowledge of physical reality is so much that we have to presume that the so-called inanimate physical objects may have after all a 'life' of their own and that it is only a matter of stirring up their 'soul'?

At yet another level there has been a growing awareness that the world view of modern physics is inconsistent with the nature of modern society with its fragmentation and conflicts. There is so little of harmony in the society of man and so much of tension and conflict, the parts tearing at each other and almost jeopardising the whole! Techniques and technologies are only handmaids of science and they cannot take over the business of ordering human affairs; for the limitations or science are only increased in a multiplier effect in its applications.

Robert Oppenheimer's statement that 'the physicist had touched sin' has to be understood in that light. The arrogance and certitude which techniques assume leading to the defeat of humanity, the ignoring of the inevitable complementarity of scientific truth and the truth of man's being on the planet and his becoming, both as an individual and as a member in the intricate web or society, the I and Thou relationship. Sin, shorn of its theological overtones, is basically the creator of *hubris* which leads to nemesis. The other face of sin is pride, the conceit of having the key to all knowledge, all power, all enlightenment.

Thus gone are the days of that supreme confidence in the power of the human mind to unravel all the mysteries of nature. In fact nature is now seen to be a strange amalgam of the object over there and also inside of us. Eddington's telling metaphor makes it only crystal clear: "we had found a strange foot-print on the shores of the unknown. And lo! it is our own". It is thus man confronting himself all alone, once again. But what a far cry it is from the Cartesian dictum 'I think, therefore I am'. Here it is 'I think, therefore we exist'. The metaphor of togetherness, of warf and woof, of yin and yang, of purusha and prakriti, thus extends to the concept of the ultimate complementarity of all nature and the entire Universe.

Coupled with this new humility in the physical sciences and this new awareness of the ultimate mystery of the space-time continuum there is an even greater awareness as to how inadequate is our knowledge of the laws governing individual life and social relationships. Perhaps we know a lot more of the outer space than the inner space of man, his individual life and his togetherness with others. Death still remains a mystery and the great unknown and the progress in opening up the secrets of extra sensory perception only beckons to newer realms of the unknown frontiers of the mind.

Science is thus getting humanised. It is coming back to the essential human dimension, the ultimate concept of togetherness.

Once again we may turn to a statement of Einstein: "I feel such a sense of solidarity with all living things that it does not matter to me where the individual begins and ends. There is nothing in the world which I could not dispense with at a moment's notice". And that has a strange *resonance* in the stoicism of Mahatma Gandhi's statement—when asked by Louis Fischer (as he was hoeing the garden) as to what he would do if he was told that he was going to die the same evening—that he would continue hoeing the garden.

Death holds no terror in either of the circumstances: when one has an implicit faith in a god or a supreme power and a conviction that not even a leaf falls from a tree without his knowledge or direction; and also when one has a perception of the ultimate togetherness of all life and therefore death becomes only a rite of passage from one mode of being or existence to another in the infinite orchestration of events that is the universe.

And today in the eyes of science, as James Jeans once put it, "the universe is more like a thought than a machine"! This is why it is so much more human. Shorn of its conceit, its earlier pride and its certainties for it the universe has the fleeting nature of a thought and yet all its uniqueness and grandeur.

There is now a new convergence between religion and science, between matter and mind, between body and soul, between individual and society. An awareness that only together they may mean something and not in binary opposition. The quest for ultimate truth which is the essence of religion is also the abiding preoccupation of all scientific enquiry. And the truth that moves the stars and planets and is responsible for their appearance and disappearance is also the truth that regulates the life and death of cells in the human body and the birth and death of societies and civilizations. There is need, therefore, for a unified theory of man, society and the universe and that theory is ultimately to be one of a total complementarity.

Science today is thus very much wearing a human face and exploring anew the meaning of being on this ancient earth.

With that newer questions of man's relationship to nature, to others in society and to the universe as a whole have also been raised. They are disturbing questions indeed and they comprehend almost all the fields of human knowledge and endeavour. But primarily they relate to ecology and harmonious relation with nature; with the possibilities of alternatives in education, health and housing; and a new approach to man's socio-economic environment.

Time was when man lived in complete harmony with nature. Even when he was no longer a forest-dweller or dependent on food gathering and hunting, and had taken up settled cultivation as the primary mode of economic sustenance, this was the dominant human relationship with nature. Man depended on it, revered it and used it for economic purposes. It was a relationship of harmony based on equality and symbiosis. But the new conceit acquired by over confident and rapid scientific advances made man assume that he was the master over nature and almost its sole exploiter. That natural resources were exhaustible and needed to be used with care and with an eye on recycling was forgotten. Man, the *homo sapien*, man the *homo luden* or man the player was becoming man, the waste-maker. It was no longer only conspicuous consumption. It was also conspicuous waste-making, turning out million and millions of tons of garbage which you did not know where to dump. It was no longer only 'black country' with chimney smoke; it was now acid rain. Miles and miles of tropical rain-forest, and forests in temperate climate were vanishing by indiscrimate felling. No, not to turn out books and paper and expand human knowledge; but to produce disposable garbage of *ad hoc*, topical information that grew irrelevant even as they were garnered and disseminated, that were almost as disposable as toilet paper. The birds were vanishing and Rachel Carson had written *The Silent Spring*, when no birds sing even in that royal season. Insecticide and pesticide spray had almost created panic situations regarding man and his food habits. Ecological disasters threatened all countries whether rich or poor, highly developed or underdeveloped or developing. For poverty, like affluence, had its own brand of pollution. In fact poverty was itself a pollution. Millions slept on pavements in bursting metropolitan connubrations in the East. Millions defecated in the open, drank water that was not potable and a sure source of health hazard. Millions lived, as they died, without knowing the plenitude of the earth and the fecundity of its resources. Cities in the West were choked with traffic, and the emissions from automobiles and factories which made the air almost unsuitable to breathe. Air, water, earth—the gifts of nature—were being polluted beyond a point and it was, to a large context, the ultimate result of scientific and technological advancement. The United Nations was concerned and that was reflected in the volume *One Earth: The Care and Maintenance of a Small Planet*. The need for urgently finding a balance between man and his environment was emphasised. Economic growth, industrialisation and urbanisation had thus destroyed the age-old balance between man and nature and to a large extent science was behind it. Ancient cultures revered the earth, for it was the mother, the giver of bounties. It gave food, sustained man and when dead he returned to her bosom. The Earth-mother motif was a dominant motif in the literature, art, belief-systems of the ancient societies. There was a fresh need to go back to nature, to that harmonious relationship.

And in health and education there were those who talked of deschooling society and medical nemesis. Not that science was responsible for the alleged authoritarian temper or the lack of concern with man and his world but it was an education that was no more in tune with the true spirit of science: the quest for meaning, constant questioning of assumptions and a childlike wonder in looking on this ancient earth and its myriad natural and man-made treasures. Instead it had bred narrow formalisms, doctrines, certainties which were not being tested constantly. There was also the linkage of such an educational system with democratic values. *The Pedagogy of the Oppressed* by Paulo Freire raised this very basic question of value.

And Ivan Illich asked why is it we are spending so much more on public health than in earlier centuries and we were no healtheir. . Why is it that newer forms of killer diseases such as AIDS, which is the plague of the present century, emerging on the scene? Is it because we were destroying the human balance, in this case the natural balance in human sexuality? Was it not also born out of that overall conceit which made one feel to almost beyond death except due to old age, the conviction that there was a cure for all diseases that afflict man? Health, after all, is not merely freedom from disease. It is a positive state of the body and the mind. And what of the increasing suicides and murders, the rapes and the riots that plague modern cities? Mental health is becoming an increasing preoccupation the world over.

Turner spoke of housing as a verb. It was meant to convey the idea that the house you lived in shaped you and your life, your values and your attitudes. It was not just a space where you lived. That speaks volumes against the urban jungles of concrete and steel that isolates men into individual prison houses unconnected to a neighbourhood and a sense of a community of shared destinies. If we are to create once again what Erich Fromm calls *The Sane Society* we must rediscover the roots of our togetherness and understand that science has also to subserve this basic goal of togetherness in society. The web of community living.

That is linked to the question of the kind of developmental goals society pursues. Is culture and man at the core of all development? Is culture looked upon as the centre-piece or merely as an instrumentality? Are the economic relationships between groups in a society such that it ensures equality and fraternity? Does the State pursue goals in science which are based on these priorities in our post-modern society?

Modern society and the modern world that came into being in the wake of the Renaissance are fast vanishing. The new post-modern world, the new post-modern social order that are emerging have to be reconciled to the new realities of the blind alley to which reason, science and technological advances have led us despite all the positive gains they have brought in. Science has to subserve the basic purpose of creating a human world, a world where man remains at the centre and the machine does not take over, where we are in harmony with nature, with the self, with others in society and the whole universe. For in a true sense, no man is an island. And science cannot afford to be amoral any longer. It has a say on the question of human survival and human balance. It has to make possible the unending renewal of man's capacity to dream. It should also know the secret how not to allow dreams to turn into nightmares. It has to wear a human face and not a robot-like mask. It has to be humanised and that alone would be the most basic change in the 'structure of consciousness' as the post-modern society of man moves on into the twenty-first century.

# 20 | The Ecstasy of Love and Communitas: A Note on Jagannath Culture

It was 1950. I was going on thirteen. And we made the long journey to Srikshetra. About twenty of us from our village for the Ratha Jatra. The journey was incredibly difficult. Buses, trains, platforms—everything was crowded. It was even difficult to get a foot-hold and often I felt cramped, choked, breathless, afraid that I may get lost. My uncle had advised me to fix my mind on Jagannath ('Call to your mind His dark round eyes') and all these troubles would vanish and I would feel them no more. Renegade that I was, the push and the pull, the stink and the humid heat in the multitude were all that remained, howsoever hard I tried to imagine and call to my mind the dark eyes of the Lord. But most of my villagers, and in fact most others I saw in the train, in the crowded platforms waiting for days on end to return home, or on the main road at Puri scrambling for a view of the Lord on the chariot—they did not seem to notice the miseries, the inconveniences around. Their faces were lit up by a strange ecstasy that was indeed baffling to me. What Rilke called 'the circumspection of human gesture' had perhaps given place to the mystery of intimacy where one lets things—and oneself—be and the multiplicity of life's processes either do not exist or vanish into the background. In one sweep of the imagination one belongs, one is.

Twenty years later, I saw the other day the *neem* tree-trunks loaded on bullock carts and wrapped in red-silk on their way to Srikshetra for the Lord's *Navakalevara*, the taking on of the New Body. The *daitapatis*, the *Deulakarans*, *Viswabasu* and the other temple servants, everybody was around. They were reenacting a complex symbolism; a legend that was perhaps truer than any truth or reality. They were undergoing a ritual process that was only partly religious. It was mostly psychological, a part of the collective unconscious. The villagers on the roadside were doing obeisance to the sacred wood, brought from somewhere in the depth of the forest around Kakatpur and the sea. The tree-trunks that bear a number of symbols. Not any ordinary tree. The gods will be given a new body, the body is mutable, liable to laws of decay and dissolution and even the gods are not immune from it. After all, Lord Jagannath, the Lord of the Universe, is like any other human being. He follows a daily routine, brushes teeth, washes his face, takes food at different times of the day, dresses differently for different occasions seasons and festivals, is put to sleep by by the lilting tune of the *devdasis* singing from the *Gita Govind*, visits his mother's sister's house and even suffers from heat-fever during the summer months. Yet this humanised god is the Lord of the Universe, his round dark eyes the eternal symbol of time and mutability, a hope for *moksa* to the devoted soul, an object celebrated in numerous poems of exquisite lyricism right from seventh century onwards.

## *Irrelevance of Historiography*

To the students of comparative religion and philosophy the temple as a socio-economic and religious institution and the so-called cult of Jagannath have been subjects of fascinating study. Here is a subject in which myth, legend, history and philosophy have got inextricably mixed. As religion and philosophy Jagannath cult is said to be a splendid synthesis of Hinduism, Buddhism, Jainism and Tantric rites. The black, white and yellow colours of the Trinity—Jagannath, Balabhadra and Subhadra respectively, are shown as the synthesis of the different groups of mankind, the white Europeans, the black Africans and the yellow Mongoloids. Jagannath has also been looked upon as Krishna, Rama, Buddha, Narayana, all in one. He has also been identified with the Mahayan Buddhism's Surya and the Brahma of Advaita Vedanta. Scholars have sought to trace his evolution from a Saivite one-piece lingam of blue-stone to a Brahminic

Trinity through symbolic representations of the Buddhistic three jewels or *Tri-ratnas*, namely Buddha, Dhamma and Sangha.

The antiquity of the place itself, Puri has been the subject of considerable historical research. From the middle of 7th century of the Christian era Puri has been a place of considerable cultural and religious significance. Indravuti, the founder of the Vajrajana sect of Buddhism, and his sister Lakshmikara were closely associated with Puri. Indravuti's monumental work in sanskrit *Jnanasiddhi* begins with an invocation to Jagannath who is said to have been a manifestation of the Buddha. Even prior to this as a *Tirtha*, a place of ancient learning and religious worship, it finds mention in the *Vanaparva* of the *Mahabharata* and a number of Puranas such as *Kurma Purana*, *Narada Purana*, *Padma Purana* and the *Utkal Khanda* of *Skanda Purana*.

Sankaracharya (788-820 A.D.) came and stayed at Puri at the height of his eminence as the spokesman of a revived Brahminism. Tradition has it that he defeated the eminent Buddhist scholars of the place in arguments before a vast concourse of learned men and established the *Govardana Pitha* which came to be recognised as one of the four Pithas of the Hindus in the four corners of India. He proclaimed Jagannath and Buddha as identical with the great Brahminical god Purushottama. Consequent on this assimilation and the establishment of a Pitha as Jagannath-Puri, there was a great revival of Sanskrit learning and scholarship at the place. According to the temple-chronical *Madala Panji*, the images of Sri Sankara and his disciple Sri Padmapada which had been installed on the jewelled-throne inside the temple for worship were removed from there only during the rule of Divyasinha Deva-II, king of Puri (1773-1798 A.D.). An entry in the Maihara inscription placed in the 10th century and found in the Sarasvati temple on a hillock near village Maihara in Madhya Pradesh speaks of the worship of Sri Purushottama on the sea-shore of Udra or Orissa and how this was the centre of religious worship for millions of Hindus.

### *Creative Eclecticism*

The existing temple was constructed at the time of Chodagangadeva around 1112 A.D. Orissa was already a powerful State and more than once successfully repulsed the Muslim invasion from north and east via Bengal. The old dilapidated temple was thus replaced only in 12th century A.D. Legend has it that this is the fourth temple on the same site. The study of Vedic literature and Puranas was in full swing at Puri by the time of Anangabhima Deva-II (1211-1238 A.D.). By this time Sri Ramanujacharya had visited Puri and under the impact of his visit and his preachings Chodaganga had become a convert to Vaishnavism thus changing the saivite, "Parama Maheswar" epithet that was current for nearly six centuries till then. Ramanuja also established a Math which still goes by his name. Besides, his disciple Govinda also established the Emar Math which is the most celebrated Math in Orissa's history. Vishnu Swami, another Vaishnava preacher from South India, also visited Puri by the second half of the twelfth century and established a Math after his name. The last to come was the eminent Madhvacharya or Ananda Tirtha. There is plenty of epigraphic evidence of the visit of these Hindu preachers and savants to Puri almost within a century (1112-1212 A.D.). Eminent historians and epigraphists like Kedarnath Mahapatra have, therefore rightly held that by the middle of the thirteenth century Puri had become the greatest centre of Hindu religion and philosophy, the most important centre for learned philosophical discourses and the final authority to decide on the complex questions of ritual, liturgy or the meanings to be assigned to existing philosophical texts. As a matter of fact the *Padma Purana* mentions how no new faith, systems of worship or religious ritual could be accepted by the Pandits all over India 'unless it got the approval of *Mukti Mandapa*, the supreme assembly of the learned Pandits at Puri'.

Sri Chaitanya is said to have stayed at Puri for eighteen long years till his death in 1533 A.D. and poets and scholars from Orissa and Bengal flocked to Puri. It was at this time that the poet of Oriya Bhagabat, Atibadi Jagannath Dasa, the author of Jagamohan Ramayana, Sri Balarama Dasa and many others lived and wrote at Puri.

Despite the Muslim invasion since 1568 A.D. after the death of Gajapati Prataparudra Deva, Puri continued to be the centre of Hindu religion and philosophy till the advent of the British into Orissa in 1803 A.D. Gajapati Ramachandra Deva who re-installed the images of the Trinity by driving away the muslim invaders from the city in 1575 A.D. and renovated the temple is popularly referred to as the 'Second Indradyumna' as a mark of honour to the legendary founder of the temple and the deities, who goes by that name.

### *Mythology and Communitas*

Jagannath is thus a splendid synthesis of not only the different schools of thought in Hinduism but has also assimilated to it concepts and 'core-thoughts' of Buddhism, Jainism and Tantra. This spirit of integration, this eclecticism is even apparent in the architectural style of the existing temple. The entrance halls called Jagamohan have the structural uniqueness of the Gopurams of South India, the hall-mark of the Dravidian style of architecture. The main temple, the *sanctum sanctorum* on the other hand, has distinctive characteristics of the North Indian Nagara style of architecture.

It would, however, be wrong to characterise the religious ceremonies or philosophical ideas surrounding Jagannath worship as Jagannath cult. This phrase has, no doubt, been popularly used by most scholars. Scholars outside India have also generally adopted this version. For example, the German Indologist Hermann Kulke calls his book *Jagannatha Cult and Gajapati Kingship* in which he explores the mechanism of legitimization of Indian Kingship. In collaboration with late Miss Eschmann and G.C. Tripathi, Kulke has also done another volume on *The Cult of Jagannath* and *The Regional Tradition of Orissa.*

It is, however, necessary to realise that this is not a cult in the narrow limited sense of a school of thought or a system of rituals or liturgies. It has never been sought to be codified as a cognitive or philosophical structure. If it has a looseness of organisation as a system of philosophy, if its liturgical or religious concepts have not been seen against the backdrop of any particular Hindu sect or sects to assess its deviations and differences from them, it is because, like Hinduism, it is more of a cultural matrix than a systematic school of philosophy or religion. It is in this sense that Jagannath cult is not a religion or a philosophy but is a broad mythology of culture. The mythic process is a learning device in which the unintelligible and the random are reduced to the intelligible and a pattern, howsoever complex. It is, as Pierre Maranda says, "essentially the investigation of the culture-conditioning mechanisms that mould ethnic cognitive systems."

If it is a system of rituals then it is based on ritual as anti-structures, a syndrome of symbol that embraces almost the whole gamut of human emotions and endeavours. The Car Festival perhaps symbolises this *Liminal* phase of the ritual-system, in which the all powerful Gajapati King sweeps the area in front of the Chariots before the swirling multitude and the Lord of the Universe leaves the cloistered seclusion of the dimly-lit *sanctum sanctorum*, the litanies of the nearly secret forms of aristocratic worship, to sit on the wooden chariots in full view of the humble and the lowly and listen to their strange orchestra private prayers and supplications. This is indeed a form of supreme *Communities*, an egalitarian relationship between persons stripped of status and property. The god of the elite, of sacred *mantras* becomes the god of the masses, each praying in his own way, soliciting, surrendering abusing, supplicating in his own private anguished self. This is thus humility and communitas combined in the most elegant manner and leads to a kind of status-reversal unique in the history of religion and philosophy. It gives a recognition to the essential and generic human bond without which there could be no society. Liminality, as Prof. Victor Turner explains, "implies that the high could not be high unless the low existed, and he who is high must experience what it is like to be low. For individuals and groups, social life is a type of dialectical process that involves successive experience of high and low, communitas and structure, homogeneity and differentiation, equality and inequality." (*The Ritual Process*, p. 97). The achievement of a degree of statuslessness by abolishing in one sweep of a symbolism all the multiple personal, group and class identity is, perhaps, the most significant aspect of Jagannath culture. It is based on a concept of submissiveness and silence that lifts *grace* to the level of a *mutual contract* between the god-head and the individual. The latter has a prior claim on the god-head. As a matter of fact the more lowly the individual, the more urgent and pressing his tragic condition, the greater is his demand on the supreme Lord. And this communitas is also established in the fact that the Lord's *Mahaprasad* can be taken from the same *Kudua* by the Brahmin priest and the untouchable. And there is no left-over so far as Mahaprasad is concerned which is thus sacrament with a difference. The menu prepared in the massive kitchen has elements of the 'folk'. Even today potato and sugar have no place in it. As Dr. Mansinha puts it, 'Jagannath's daily menu includes cakes made out of contemptible rice-bran and dishes of the commonest pot-herbs such as only the poorest in Orissa usually take. Further, even though Jagannath was the imperial god of the Gajapatis in historical times his chariots were never drawn by either the militia, the hired labour or the elephant. Instead it is the millions of devotees who pull the ropes of the chariot and give a poignant expression to the concept of communitas that is the essence of Jagannatn culture.

The images of the Trinity are made out of sacred neem-tree and these trees are carefully selected in the years when there is a renewal of the images or *Navakalebara.* The wooden images are reminiscent of their probable primitive origin. Legend has it that the tribal chieftain Viswabasu originally worshipped the lord as Nilamadhava and Vidyapati, the Brahmin emissary sent by him deceived Lalita, the daughter of the chieftain, and stole the Tribal god. When the Lord vanished and king Indradyuman was in anguish he had a dream that a log of wood would come floating on the eastern sea-board and out of that His image will be created. There is also the other legend how the carpenter was locked up in a room to work on the wooden images and he had requested that until twenty-one days the doors of the room should not be opened. When the sound of chisel and hammer thinned down to a near-silence the queen could bear it no longer and afraid that the aged carpenter may be dead or dying she had the doors opened by force only to find that the carpenter had vanished and the three incomplete wooden images were there. This is another symbolic representation of the idea that the universal god as an ideal dream is never fully realised in this world. The tribal origin of Jagannath is thus a distinct possibility. Even today worship of trees and flowers are common among the primitive tribes of India. New flowers on Sal and Mahul trees are occasions for ritual worship among the Mundas and the Santals. Many of the festivals like the *Santal Baha* festival (flower festival) are vegetation and fecundity ceremonies. Among the Savaras of Southern Orissa also there is a form of tree worship. The *Sarna* or the sacred grove at the end of the village where most worships take place is itself an evidence of the reverence for tree in primitive cultures. J. G. Erazer in his *The Golden Bough* has cited numerous illustrations of this worship of trees in the religious history of the Aryan race. "At Upsala, the old religious capital of Sweden, there was a sacred grove in which every tree was regarded as divine. The heathen slaves worshipped trees and groves. Among the Lithuanians, prior to their conversion to Christianity the worship of trees was prominent" (pp. 145-46 of the abridged edition)

### *Primitive Origins and the Fury of Words*

The spirit of primitive reverence for life and communitas so characteristic of Jagannath culture is nowhere manifest in a more moving form than in the hundreds of prayer-songs the *Jananas* and *Bhajans*, dedicated to the Lord and composed in his honour by the poets of Orissa in different periods of history. Some of them like Banamali Das and Bhaktacharan of 18th century, the leper Dinakrushna of *Rasakallola* fame in 17th century, Gopal Krishna and Kavisurya (19th century) Abhimanyu (18th century) and the Muslim poet Salabega (17th century) are well known in the literary annals of Orissa, and they have composed *Jananas* and *Bhajans* which are really the heart-throb of millions of Oriyas everywhere. Besides the more well known, there are unknown or lesser known poets whose poems are a part of the national culture, a distinct part of the cultural ethos. Who, for example, in Orissa would not know at least a stanza from the 17th century wandering begger-poet Saria Vika's prayer-song:

> *'O' my tired mind let us go*
> *and see His round eyes*
> *and bathe our own eyes*
> *in the mandala of the navel of the conch*

or the soul-stirring songs of Salabega:

*He has no hands, no feet,*
*who will keep him tied?*
*'O' thou mad elephant of the blue mountain*
*rush in and despoil the lotus-forest of my anguish.*

Or the mood of utter resignation to the Lord in Banamali's famous lines:

*O Jagannath*
*I ask nothing of you*
*not wealth nor men*
*I ask only a cubit from your Saradha Bali*

(Saradha bali is the bed of the legendary dried-up river Malini that used to flow between Badadanda and Gundicha pavilion)

The songs are numerous and almost all of them are composed in moving tunes. They have become a part of the collective unconscious of the people. There is rarely another instance when songs composed over successive centuries have for themselves enshrined or etched in the popular imagination and given them a poignancy and a meaningfulness seldom available to religious literature of the academic variety. The songs are hummed and sung almost everywhere and on almost every occasion by beggars, by sadhus, by learned Pandits, by the old and the young, by scholars, musicians and even by the modern dilettants. They are not only excellent as music, they are excellent even as poetry, a poetry that comes from the heart of human suffering, dedication, brotherhood and love. A Shakespearean character says, "I understand the fury in your words but not the words." It is this spiritual fury in these prayer songs that infuses them with a quality of timelessness and poignancy.